CHRISTIANA'S SECRET:

The Lost Treasure of Dead Man's Gulch

By Ray Golden

Golden Ray Distributers

WWW.GOLDENRAYDISTRIBUTORS.COM

Golden Ray
Distributers

WWW.GOLDENRAYDISTRIBUTORS.COM

Printed in the United States of America

Book Design: Linda W. Rigsbee

Proudly Printed by:
The Print Connection
www.PrintConnectionDenver.com

CHAPTER ONE

L ittle did I know in the wee hours of that August morning in 1987 the incredible and exasperating journey I was about to embark upon. Still dark, at about 3 a.m., I was lying awake in bed when my attention was drawn to the upstairs hallway. I faced it directly from the master bedroom in our Victorian-style home in Colorado Springs. The company I worked for as sales manager had been sold and I was without a job. My wife, Meredith, was pregnant and days from giving birth to our daughter, Mariah. Sleep was the last thing on my mind.

At the end of and to the right of the hallway was the bedroom Meredith had made into a nursery for the baby. Her intuition assured her the baby was going to be a girl, and there certainly was no second guessing on my part. Meredith had been trained and was talented in the art of drawing and painting. She had painted three of the walls in that room with famous Disney characters. On the fourth wall, she painted a baby's crib and an angel, together with the words *And you shall dance in the velvet sky and the silvery stars shall twinkle and dream sweet dreams as over their beams your footfalls softly twinkle.*

As you read on, you might accuse me of dreaming. That is, unless you're of a persuasion to believe in apparitions. In fact, there are at least two people, and possibly one dog who's seen the same ghost in this house, which was built in 1874. I'm not sure what the dog thought; she just barked at the ceiling. These two persons of upstanding character have both given the same description of their vision of this lady ghost. They saw her in the same part of the house, upstairs. They weren't coached by me in any way. I know you might have a tendency to think that, if you don't believe. Neither of them knew of the encounter I had this summer morning; a memory that has been permanently imprinted in my mind. Furthermore, I exhibit no tendency to expand on dreams without the aid of alcohol and spirits of embellishment, although I do admit to enjoying a cold beer as much as any other person. Quarts of beer were a staple in our family's home when it could be afforded. Meredith can attest that was not the case that morning.

As I lay on the west side of the bed with the light of the television pulsing in and out, complimented by a Mickey Mouse night light in the upstairs bathroom, I saw something move in a blur down the hall. From the corner of my eye, I could see a light I'd never seen before and the detail of a woman coming out of the baby's room. She turned left toward our bedroom and quickly traversed the hallway and into our room. As I watched intently, my thought was *Oh, this is interesting!* I clearly observed her appearance: dark hair highlighted with grey, an older face, but no wrinkles or age lines. She wore a dark Victorian-style dress with lace at the top of the neck line. I could see a long necklace with something like a gold coin attached to it. *Oh no*, I thought. It was at that moment I remembered her. My life had almost been taken from me many years before when I saw her during my boyhood years. Memories rushed to my brain. I got goose bumps and my arm hairs stood up and danced. The flash of a forgotten reality took hold of my spirit and shook it like the swirl of Rocky Mountain wind.

It was on the banks of the Connecticut River, next to a dam and a waterfall in a little town called Thompsonville. My cousin Rebecca and I were going fishing for shad for Grandma Pearl's dinner that night. She had given birth to eighteen children and had taught us well how to fish. She needed all the help she could get come dinner time. Rebecca and I were two cousins of over a hundred grandchildren; our fathers were brothers. Our parents were off on a trip to New York and we didn't mind staying at Grandma's to go fishing. After all, we were becoming pros with our little fishing poles and hooks with colored beads attached. Before our parents left, my dad said, "Charlie, you stay away from that waterfall. You know how many people have drowned there. There will be hell to pay when I get back if you get hurt."

"Okay, Dad," I cocked my head in a sheepish tilt, looking up to him with my blue eyes as if to say *you know you love me, Dad*.

"Rebecca, you take care of Charlie," Uncle Fran told her with the look of pride he always displayed. She was a whole year older than me; she was nine then and I was eight.

After instructions from grandma on how many fish she

needed, we scooped up our gear and started our hike through the back of the schoolhouse yard and down to the river bank. Lots of other cousins, brothers, sisters, aunts and uncles played ball in the farmer's pasture next door. There was Roger, Donnie, Shelly, Kathy, Gary, Scott, Debbie, Robbie, Ronnie, Don, Cindy, Alan, Wayne, Rene Jr., Rickie, George, Johnny, Eddie, Rene Sr., Barbara, Leona, Bobby, Lorraine, Lucille, Judy, Betty, Mary, Freddie, Tommy and little Ray. It was a Saturday and my brother Donnie was teasing the bull tied up to a chain. He yelled out, "Charlie, watch out for those sink holes!"

Grandpa George bought an old schoolhouse to have enough room for his ever-growing family. It didn't have running water or much of a heating system at first, except for an old stove. The shingles were old and worn and the staircase was uncovered. The downstairs was all one room with a kitchen to one side and lots of old chairs with a big table in the middle. Upstairs were two rooms, a big one for all of the kids with lots of cots for beds and one for the married couple. It was comfy, though, with the sound of laughter always spilling out of the exterior walls. What a great family, the likes of which I have yet to see duplicated. There were always chickens running loose, waiting for Grandma's axe and the dinner table. Lots of rhubarb also awaited in the yard for Grandma's pie-making moods. The smell of tobacco was always present in the air in the summer from the growing fields nearby. Best of all, the candy store was close by.

As we neared the river, the sun bounced off the waves and crashed into the river bank. A small motorboat with two men and a boy were trolling out toward the center of the river, which was quite wide in places. The mud was squishy and our little feet sank down deep in some places. Just ahead, a water snake crossed in front of us. We stopped suddenly and hugged; we didn't like snakes much. Starting out again, I tipped my baseball cap down over my left eye to avoid the hot afternoon sun, and Rebecca assured me that there probably wouldn't be any more snakes to worry about that day.

We picked up our pace when we could hear the sound of water. When we got close enough to see the waterfall, Rebecca said, "We had better stop here, Charlie. Remember what your dad told you about this place."

"Well," I replied, "we can catch more fish down there because they're trying to jump over the waterfall."

"All right, Charlie, but remember it'll be your hide if something bad happens."

"Okay, let's take a chance. Grandma needs those fish." We settled in a nice spot in front of a big boulder next to the tremendous fall of water. The noise was so loud we could barely hear each other talk. Birds came and went as they fed off the leftovers on the rocks from previous fish cleanings. A slight breeze wafted across the river from the Windsor Locks side. Pollywogs swam in little pools at the edge of the river. It was such a pleasant day, and yet an eerie feeling had come over me. There was a presence there I didn't know or understand.

We started catching fish right away. First Rebecca caught one, and then me. I was having a blast. We had caught half a dozen nice ones before an hour went by. We were proud and couldn't wait to show Grandma what we'd caught. We thought we'd try for six more before it got too late. That was about the time gloomy clouds came rolling over us and the wind picked up. A strange mist colored the waterfall, with just enough sun peeking through to glitter off of a shiny object which I could see behind the waterfall. It might be a penny, I thought, or a gold coin. Then I changed my mind and thought that it might be too big for a penny. I was always finding coins. It seemed like every place I'd been I could find at least a penny. By a nice coincidence, that was exactly how much Red Hot Candy was. I thought I was a lucky kid. Years later, my dad, Donald, said to me, "Charlie, you've always been so lucky all of your life that you could step in a pile of you-know-what and come out smelling like a rose every time." Looking back, I think he was right. By now, fish weren't the first thing on my mind.

I said to Rebecca, "Do you see that? Look how it shines! I think it might be a whole gold dollar in there. It must've fallen over the dam."

"Charlie, don't you even think about it. That's too dangerous!" Rebecca replied with fright in her eyes.

"No, no, I can do it," I said. "I'll just go behind the wall of water on the rocks. You know how athletic I am. If it makes you feel better, you can tie that fishing line on to me so you can pull me back if you need to."

"Well, I guess that might be okay if you're real careful—and if we can stop by Hartley's store on the way home and get some candy." The fright left her eyes with the thought of those candy jars.

A smile crept over my face as I traversed the rocks leading behind the waterfall. As I entered the darkened void between the water and the rock face wall, a pair of dragonflies escaped from within. Their wings fluttered hurriedly as they danced their way in between tiny streams of water falling in a random craziness, like raindrops dripping off the top of an umbrella. The rocks below my feet were stained with remains of decaying shad fish that hadn't survived the treacherous leap over the dam. The noise became more and more deafening, and the light was disappearing fast. The moss growing on the rock was so slippery that I nearly fell with every step. I was thinking about the tongue lashing this crazy stunt was going to get for me as a reward.

Now I couldn't see the coin any longer. I tried yelling to Rebecca, but there was no response. "Can you still see it? Can you see me?" I yelled in vein, but was sure she couldn't hear me. A chill washed over me and I became soaking wet. The water dripped down my forehead and into my eyes. As I wiped my eyes with my Barney Rubble handkerchief I thought I heard a whisper. It couldn't be, though. The sound of water was too loud to hear a whisper. Yet I heard it again. "This way," the woman's voice said. I was startled and quickly looked over to my right. I could see a woman; the same woman I would see in my home in the future. That same gold coin hung from her necklace. I took one step backward, slipped on the moss rock, and went down into the mud. As I tried to recover, I slid farther down into the sinkhole

I was in. The water covered my face. I could see the lady beckon to me as I grabbed at the rocks above me. The rock I got hold of slid down and a terrible pain shot into my brow. In my dizziness I saw her fade back into the gap in the rocks. The pain of loneliness was suddenly greater than that of my bruise.

I stopped sinking in the mud at the last possible moment. The fishing line I was tied to caught on something. I heard the sound of thunder cracking through the waterfall. "Boy, I'm in a pickle," I said to myself. Now with the squishy mud slipping in between my toes, I tried kicking my feet to push out, but my effort was to no avail. I couldn't get any traction no matter how hard I tried. Blood ran down onto the corner of my lip. The dripping water cleansed me just as fast and a cringing pain from my forehead blinded my concentration. I tried to think my way out. The water rose and choked me, cutting off my ability to breathe. I was losing hope. Just then a fisherman's rope flopped down on me from the top of the dam. I grabbed it quick for the sake of my life. As I pulled at it, I freed myself from the suction of the mud, slowly pulling my way up and out of the temporary grave.

Back up on the rocks I noticed the lady one more time through the water drops. She wore a wide grin and a discernable look of satisfaction. I moved rapidly to escape without any more thought of the coin that had tempted me so much. On the return to daylight, Rebecca ran over to me. "Charlie, what happened? I'm so glad you're safe! You'd better not do that again or I swear that I'll never talk to you again!"

"Don't worry, I won't," I assured her with a deep breath,

knowing that I'd almost been a dead duck. I didn't mention the ghost to anyone for fear of the ridicule I'd surely face. We returned to Grandma's with all of the fish. The only thing we endured that night were questions about how Charlie got wet and muddy with a bruised forehead.

"What did you do, Charlie, go in after the fish?" my brother Roger asked with a chuckle.

"That's all right, guys. Laugh all you want, but who brought dinner home?" I said, glancing over at the big smile on Rebecca's face. I was proud of my escape, but knew nothing of who my saver was.

I remember going to sleep that night thinking about the mysterious ghost lady with the bright gold coin hanging from her necklace.

CHAPTER TWO

N ow, as that memory faded back into the flickering light of the TV, here she was again. I wondered if she was real. "She knows I can see her. Why is she here? She's gesturing for me to follow her. I don't understand what she wants." She turned and I saw her eyes twinkle, as if to reassure me of her good intentions. Her hair flowed as if caught in the wind, but without such a force present. Her Victorian dress barely touched the floor, and yet I could see her float under motion which I could not understand. She started back down the long hallway and then turned toward me to be sure I'd follow her. I put my slippers on to avoid the slivers in the antique wood floors. Then I tried to speak to her. "Can you understand me?" I asked. She responded with a reassuring nod of the head and a larger smile.

Well, I thought, I might as well see what this is all about. Looking back on the moment, I was never scared, yet somehow I was sure of my sanity. Then again, I was never predisposed to being afraid of anything, except snakes that is. I followed her down the hall and then down the stairs. She turned to me once more and moved into the bar I'd built in an old downstairs bedroom. The only light was from the outside porch. I could see her clearly as she beckoned me to one wall where old west photographs hung on display. Among those photos was a picture of my dad and me. It was taken on a gold panning trip he and I had taken to Dead Man's Gulch. We were standing in front of a steep cliff with a waterfall. It was then that she magically disappeared into the picture, gradually fading into the waves of water.

The room was quiet, as if nothing at all had happened. I could only wonder why she had come back into my life. Sitting on a bar stool, I poured myself a shot of Crown Royal whiskey. The occasion warranted an expensive wake-up call. I pondered what she was trying to tell me without any conclusion. I did make a vow, however, to go back to Dead Man's Gulch. I was driven by that thought until my chance came only two weeks later.

On a cloudless Saturday morning with a slight breeze in the air, Meredith came out onto the back porch where I'd been daydreaming about what might await me in those towering mountains behind Pikes Peak. "Charlie, everyone is coming over today at noon for my baby shower. What are your plans?"

"Well, this might be a good day to take Sarah for a ride in the mountains."

"Oh great, Sarah will love that." She bent down to pet Sarah, telling her, "Sarah's going for a ride today!"

Sarah jumped up and down. She knew what that word "ride" meant. Sarah was our 152-pound Great Pyrenees dog we'd adopted from the local Great Pyrenees Savior Society. I'd often said she was the smartest dog I'd ever known. She was as big as a bear and yet very mellow, with big brown eyes that looked up at you and begged for a treat. When we spoke to her, she would raise her eyebrows as if she understood what we were saying. Excitement rushed through my brain as adrenaline encouraged my sense of adventure. I hurriedly went to the shed and began packing a few things I might need. Dad's pickax, which he'd left behind, and a fold-up camp shovel. I was already mapping out a plan. I thought I'd dig in that area, but not knowing for what. Of course, I also packed my fold-up rope which I never went into the mountains without. Meredith made a lunch for Sarah and me, insisting that I be careful. "Now Charlie, don't you give me anything to worry about."

"We're going for a nice ride and a little treasure hunt," I called out to Sarah, "Ready for a ride?" She jumped up and down with excitement, then barked and ran to the door.

Meredith and I laughed as we always did when Sarah was so happy. I grabbed my Red Sox baseball cap and a windbreaker on the way out the door. Then I kissed Meredith goodbye.

"Have a good time and come home before dark, okay?" she pushed for reassurance.

"I hope you get some nice gifts for the baby today." I opened the Jeep's rear hatch so Sarah could jump into the back. She was too big for me to pick up. I patted her on the head, then tossed in my backpack.

"Are you ready to go, Sarah?"

As we drove up Ute Pass and ascended Pikes Peak, I had

several flash memories of gold panning days with my dad and brothers, Roger and Donnie. My mom, Marilyn, went along as well. My friend Teddy and one of Mom's friends, Gerry, also went on prospecting trips with Sarah and me. *Those were the days,* I thought with much fondness. A single cloud hovered over the summit of the mountain like a halo. This was the same mountain that inspired the song "America the Beautiful" by Katharine Lee Bates. The mountain did appear purple and majestic at times.

A Pikes Peak Cog Railway train was starting its climb up the mountain and was packed full of tourists. A hot air balloon drifted above the railcar. Those adventurers were practicing for the balloon festival celebrated each year in Colorado Springs during Labor Day weekend. A falcon hunted from above, gliding without effort. People in cars passing us by laughed and waved at Sarah's big head sticking out of the back window as she sniffed into the breeze. The winding turns up the pass were a challenge to navigate. The trip would take about two hours, so I put a cassette tape of oldies into the stereo and enjoyed the music in tandem with the fabulous scenery.

We drove up Highway 24 past Green Mountain Falls and through the sleepy mountain town of Woodland Park. Turning north on Highway 67, it was a short distance to the town of Bailey where the South Platte River winds through densely populated mountains. As we drove over Kenosha Pass, the view of the Mosquito Range Mountains widened and become awesome. I thought about what it must have been like 128 years before and how Dead Man's Gulch got its name. Located in the mountainous region of Colorado known as South Park, it was inhabited by the Ute Indian tribe in 1859. South Park was one of many regions in Colorado where groups of prospectors searched for gold in the tributaries of the South Platte River. South Park may also have been referred to as "Bayou Salado." This area was treasured by the Utes for its abundance of game, clean spring water, and sometimes mild climate.

When the prospectors first arrived and began to hunt for game and fouled the water with their digging, the Utes felt threatened and began hunting down and killing the prospectors. During that year, it was rumored that three prospectors were caught by the Utes. Two of those men were killed and one man managed to escape to tell of the event. Two separate accounts of another massacre tell of six, then seven, prospectors who were caught and killed near Kenosha Pass. No one seemed to know which account of how many were killed was actually true. When other prospectors stumbled upon the bleached bones of the unfortunate ones, the area was named Dead Man's Gulch.

It was four years later when two German prospectors discovered a rich lode of gold somewhere up the gulch. It was rumored that they had taken out over seven thousand dollars' worth of gold in their first week. Their good fortune was short-lived, however. One died suddenly and the other left the region permanently. Since that time, many have searched for the lost German mine, but none have found it. So goes the mystery of the lost treasure of Dead Man's Gulch.

My brothers, Dad, and I panned for gold many times in that region, but it was on my last trip up here that was on my mind now. My brother Roger had returned home to Connecticut. My brother Donnie, with an endless sense of humor, moved to Georgia. He has since died on the 123rd anniversary of the shootout at the OK Corral.

Dad and I, without knowing it, went on our last trip looking for gold. Driving through the trees on a road that was a little more than a path, we came upon a tributary of the South Platte River. An old log cabin stood, sloped on its edge. Next to the cabin was an old wooden sluice box hanging by the river's edge. We became wide-eyed and excited and immediately stopped to unload our equipment. The water ran low and slow since the snow was finished with its big melt. There were places in the river that looked shallower than others.

As Dad set up our portable sluice box for action, he asked me to take the metal detector across the river to the other side where the cabin was. "Why don't you check around for buried coins and gold, Charlie. Maybe those guys buried something." As I started out, I looked for the best place to cross. I walked upstream a short distance, close to where an island was accessible, all the while looking down as I made my way through the cactus. Mountain cactus is so sharp it will go right through your shoe if you get close enough to touch it. It really hurts; I know from previous experience! I glanced to the left of the river bank where a small stream was emptying in and was stunned with what I saw: the ground where the stream and river met was yellow as if someone had colored it with a crayon!

"Dad, come quick! Look what I found!" Dad rushed over and marveled at what I'd found; he smirked like we'd just found the gates of heaven.

"Well look at that, my boy. Isn't it pretty?" Dad grinned as he sat down to admire the find we'd worked so hard and traveled so far for.

We panned out all of the gold dust, knowing we'd only found the remains of a gold vein somewhere close by. Still it was like all the gold in the world to us. Before we left with our treasure, we took a walk upstream to see what was there. As we got a mile upstream, we heard a waterfall. Getting closer, we could see the magnificent sight as the noise grew deafening. It was a beautiful view among the Aspen trees and rocks galore from the big mountain above. We looked around for more signs of gold, but with no more luck.

As we were thinking about leaving, a congenial couple out hiking with their dog asked us to take a picture of them in front of the waterfall. I did, and then they returned the favor and took one for us. We drove back home and sold our gold to a local coin shop whose owner, Jim Field, promised to buy anymore gold we might find. After Dad went back to Maine, I had the photo blown up, framed, and placed on the wall. Dad died the next year. We had found our treasure, meek as it was. It was a treasure nonetheless, and remains one of my proudest memories.

Sarah's barking brought my mind back to present day and my eyes back on the road. A large herd of elk grazed in a pasture next to Wellington Lake Road, which was the road we were driving on. As we stopped for a nature break, the only sound I could hear was the whistle of the mountain wind rushing through the canyon. Once we were back on the road and turned a few miles ahead onto the cart path-like road which I'd been on with Dad, I felt a rush of chills. The closer Sarah and I got to that special place, the more the hair on my arms stood up with anticipation of what might await us. Upon seeing the cabin, I parked the Jeep and took a deep breath, wishing Dad was with me again. I could almost hear him talking to me. This special place put my imagination on overtime. It was as if everyone was there, yet no one at all: my dad, the Ute Indians, the old gold miners, the Germans, Sarah, and maybe that special ghost.

CHAPTER THREE

There I was, though, back to reality and next to a river wondering what I was going to do now. I took the lunch Meredith made for us up to the waterfall for a picnic first. Corned beef sandwiches were a favorite of mine, and Sarah's, along with two bottles of Coors Light to wash it all down. Yes, Sarah liked beer too. As I found a semi-comfortable rock to sit on, I watched Sarah jump into the little pond next to the waterfall. I wondered what it must have been like there before the invasion of white settlers took hold forever. It was nothing I could change, so I began looking for the rest of Dad's and my treasure. As I looked at the top of the mountain, I felt sure that somewhere deep within was a vein of gold. Where was it coming from? The gold dust we found must have come from somewhere in that vast mountain. I knew it was a dangerous climb, but I thought we could do it without too much trouble.

Whistling for Sarah, I scaled the rocky edge of the mountain toward the top. Just then I heard the growl of a mountain lion. I looked up to see him perched above me, ready to strike. I didn't have time to turn and run, and feared for my life. In an instant,

Sarah jumped ahead of me and charged like a wild beast. I had never seen this part of her personality before. She pounced on the lion with her full force, knocking him off of the rocky edge and down into the pond below. Swimming out onto the muddy bank, the lion growled again back up at us, shook off, and decided to find his lunch elsewhere. I sat down on a rock, relieved, and thought about what a close encounter that was. After a few minutes, I regained my composure. Sarah and I continued our climb. There were lots of different colors of speckled rocks in this formation. There was garnet, ruby speckles, and turquoise too. Some of the rocks were jagged and sharp. The cactus again made me fearful and cautious. The small scrub oak branches gave me places to hold onto as I held Sarah's collar with my other hand. The terrain became so steep that we had to retreat in favor of a different way up the mountain.

At the bottom again and winded, I stepped back away from the giant formation and waterfall to have a better look at my challenge. The brightness of the sun disappeared to the right of the waterfall into what appeared to be total darkness. I walked closer as I saw a path behind the waterfall. I caught my breath, swallowed hard, and decided to have a look. I had done this before and barely survived, I reminded myself. Not wanting Sarah to come in with me, I said, "Stay girl." She did, but with two barks of disagreement. As I disappeared behind the falls I could hear her bark with more dissatisfaction. I knew she'd be there when I returned. We could always count on her to wait for us, even without a leash.

It was scary there now, very dark, noisy, and eerie. The little path led me far back between the rocks and the water. I lit my lighter to see whatever I could. I wasn't worried about snakes in there because I knew the altitude was way too high for them to live in. They like warmth too much and are usually found below 10,000 feet. We were up over 12,000 feet in altitude at the time. Some of the Colorado mountain peaks are as high as 14,000 feet, which is far above the tree line. There are fifty-four mountains that tall in Colorado. Trying to breathe calmly, I inched in further until I saw a gap between the rocks. Going in, I was amazed at the cozy cavern tucked in behind. "What a cool place," I said out loud. Remains of long-ago camp fires were present in the pit to the center of the cavern. I knew someone had been there before me, but maybe a long time ago. Seeing a few leftover sticks, I lit my own fire. Sensing that it was safe for Sarah, I whistled for her and she came running quickly. Sitting next to the fire, petting and talking to Sarah, I was wondering who it was that might have been here before me. Looking around at the inside rock walls, I spotted a scratching in a rock on one of the walls that seemed to be in the shape of an upward pointing arrow and what looked like a "C" scratched into the top of the arrow.

My curiosity got me going directly to that wall. Now I was intrigued. Looking up in the direction of the arrow, I could see a gap in the rock face wall directly below the top. Over to the left was a skinny ledge ascending it. I immediately started my way up to the gap and, upon arrival, could see what appeared to be a deer hide wrapped in a bundle. Reaching into the gap and grabbing hold, I realized there was something wrapped in the bundle. Quickly retreating to the fire next to Sarah with the bundle in my hand, a sense of wonder and mystery washed over me. I opened the material and was amused to find a book inside. *What a place for this*, I thought. It was an old book with a worn cloth liner and what was left of an antique pencil. There was something wrapped separately from the book. It was heavy. As I held the separate deer cloth in my hand and opened it, I saw what I thought I had seen before: it looked like the necklace and gold coin I had seen the ghost lady wear on two separate occasions. It was then I knew this was the place she had been trying to guide me to. The necklace was solid gold and roughly fashioned with a single letter M carved in it. I didn't know what it stood for, but I admired it and put it away safely in my zippered pocket. As I opened the book I could barely read the name Henry Fitsimmonds on the first page, followed by the date 1861. The next few pages had notes and maps of the mountain passes I had just driven through from Colorado Springs. The last page, with his handwriting on it, had the word *Eureka* with a circle on the map here at the waterfall. His writing stopped abruptly. Then I got another surprise. Someone else started writing on the very next page of the book. The top line read *Diary of Christiana Fitsimmonds*.

CHAPTER FOUR

The diary started out with these words: *My name is Christiana Fitsimmonds. The Ute Indian tribe that adopted me calls me by the name of Mamaci Paa. (Woman in Water), which is how I was found. I was hiding behind this waterfall after they killed the party of six men I was traveling with. One of those men was my dear brother, Henry Fitsimmonds. I am writing this diary in hopes that whoever finds it will be kind enough to give it to my descendants if they exist in your time. If you have found this writing and have the desire to do so for me, then I will be happy to trust in you and provide you with information that will guide you to a treasure of gold hidden nearby. Money is not useful to the people I live with, neither do I care for the ugliness of what it produces. I have become content now, living in this place of peace. My captors have become my family. They care for me well and with much respect. My favorite hat with the ostrich feather has led them to believe I am someone important in the white man's world; I have not dissuaded them from that thought since I was scared at first. We have plenty of food and stay busy in our daily chores. They are more delightful than cleaning a house. The wildlife is beautiful and easy to approach. The weather has been mild and comfortable. The spring water is refreshing and the pond suits my bathing needs very well. I can look after the gravesites of my brother and our companions with whom we traveled. My only regret is the loss of those dear souls, all. They were truly good men in pursuit of their dreams. They were completely surprised and overwhelmed by the Ute war party. I hold no resentment now of the Ute Indians as I understand the threat they face and why they defend their home in such a fierce way. I must return to the people; I will speak more of this tragic event upon my next visit to my secret place.*

"How could I be so lucky to find this place?" I said to Sarah.

She replied *Ruff!* I could hardly wait to turn to the next page and did so quickly.

I have returned today with the sadness of the memories of my companions, I will tell of the events of that terrible day. I was taking a bath in the pond below when the attack was sprung so quickly on my companions. They were panning for gold. My brother and his friend Jim were building a new sluice box. I heard war cries and shots pierce the air and hid behind this waterfall. It has become my place of safety the past few years. There was another waterfall in my life that served the same purpose. It was in a little town called Thompsonville, in Connecticut. That is where Henry and I are from. I played often at that waterfall as a young girl.

The warriors didn't find me at first; it was only when they discovered my female belongings and dresses did they begin looking for me. The chief's son and heir, Suu Tavaci, (One Sun) searched for me until he found me here, shivering and scared, behind this waterfall. He stared and looked me over before taking me to his father and chief,

Wacuwini Muatagoci, (Four Moons). Three winters have passed now since the massacre of my party. I mark each winter with the round rocks placed at the edge of the little pond. I use the roundest ones I can find to signify the circle of a year. I come here for solitude, for safety, and to think. I now wish to leave a record of my life here and hope someday my story can be told. I am now thirty-three years of age. I believe the year to be 1864. I will come here to write more when I can. Suu Tavaci is my husband now and will be the chief of the people. The gold necklace you have surely found here with the diary was a wedding present from him and he has carved it with the first initial of my new name. I leave it in this place with my diary to keep it safe. I wish for any descendants you may find for me to have this necklace; that is, if you are of a generous nature, which I hope with most sincerity.

I am feeling the sickness of pregnancy now. I believe this child will be born in the late fall. I must lay in many supplies while I can and fashion clothes for the baby the best I can. I am learning much from the other squaws. Their language and arts are coming to me quickly. I hope to finish this writing before your English language is a distant memory to me. I find myself thinking more and more in the Ute language. It isn't that difficult when you hear it so often.

Just then, *Crack!* I heard the sound of thunder outside of the cavern. I said to Sarah, "We have to go now before that storm traps us here."

Ruff, ruff! she replied. Colorado thunderstorms can be hellacious, and flash floods can take a life instantly. As we scurried toward the Jeep and past the pond, I counted sixteen round stones next to the pond and wondered what else I would read about in Mamaci Paa's diary. Moments later, hail started, pelting us like bullets from the sky. I knew we couldn't make it and whistled to Sarah up ahead on the trail. She was reluctant and I think her instincts told her not to go back, but she dutifully returned while barking at me and backing up. "Come on girl, we have to get to a safe place."

She led me back to the cavern. The fire was still smoldering and we were out of the horrible storm. We were safe for the moment, but I knew we would both be trapped if the storm didn't pass over quickly. It didn't, and as I sat there next to the fire, I resigned myself to a longer stay than I had planned for. I wondered what Meredith might say when I didn't return that night. I had given her a brief description of where we were going, but didn't know if she would remember exact directions. I could only hope the car didn't wash away in the flood I suspected was coming. As I went back out for a peek, I could see the water rising quickly and the trail begin to disappear. Back inside, I looked through my backpack to find one more sandwich, cookies, and a few more Sarah treats. I had a sweater packed since I had been in such storms in Colorado and knew what could come so quickly.

I sat down to think for a while. There wasn't much wood left, and I decided to save what remained in case we were still there after dark. After all, there was at least one mountain lion around somewhere, maybe close by and maybe still hungry. Getting as comfortable as possible, I lit one of the dry cigarettes in my soggy backpack and unwrapped Christiana's diary. Sarah lay down next to the warm rocks and looked up at me with those big brown eyes as if to say *uh oh!* As I turned to the next page in the diary, I noticed the heading *Diary of Mamaci Paa*. I began to read on, thinking the Ute language was taking hold as she suggested it might.

My baby is one year old now; we have survived a hard winter and attacks by scouts for the settlers this past summer. I wanted to come up here to see the yellow aspen leaves and get the rest that I most assuredly need. My baby is old enough to be cared for and fed for a short time by my friends and faithful sisters of the tribe. I have named the baby Maiku (Friendly Greeting) after the big smile on his face when he first saw his father. This life is peaceful and I have long appreciated the simple things in life. We pick as many berries as we like and never have waste. The braves in our camp work hard to provide meat for dinner and defend us with honor from our enemies. We always have a campfire and a warm tepee. The children frolic in the camp and pretend to be great hunters as the elders tell of their brave adventures in their youth. Some have great stories which I am sure they embellished just a little bit. I am enjoying life here more and more now and becoming sure I will spend the rest of my days here in contentment.

That was all the writing on that page, so I went out to take another peek at the weather. The rain was falling harder than I had ever seen in Colorado, and that's saying a lot. The river was swollen and I wondered if my car would withstand the flood or be washed away. Sarah was whining now; it was not like her. She was alert and nervous. Her ears stood straight up to hear what she could. I was alarmed as well. I had never seen her so uneasy. I huddled with her and we watched and listened. The water level in the little pond was rising up almost to the level of the cavern floor. The lightning and thunder was deafening and persistent, with one bolt striking after another. I tucked the book inside my shirt and called to Sarah with a treat from my backpack. She whined and licked the cut on my arm from the cactus. We huddled for what seemed like hours before the storm subsided. We were safe for the time being, but trapped. I knew we would have to stay the night, and maybe longer. I put the last sticks on the fire and tried to get us as comfortable as possible. We shared the backpack for the pillow and fell into a semi-sleep.

I awoke to the sunlight beaming in between the waterfall and the cavern and heard the heavy rush of water. I couldn't see out because the water level was high, and I also couldn't traverse the rock path entry. I hoped the water level would subside soon, and knew we could wait it out for a few hours before trying to get to the car. All I could do was to unsheathe the book again and read on. As I turned the page in anticipation and read the first words, my feelings were with Christiana.

This winter has been hard; it is early spring now. I have just placed another rock by the pond. The winter snows were so heavy that they have just melted completely in the last moon. The food storage is completely gone. The hunters have been away for many days looking for the elk herd which had left us for lower ground and better pastures. We are living on the new grown berries that we can find. Maiku cries with hunger and we are both weak. I fear if the braves do not return soon that we will perish.

My heart sunk as I read on. I felt the hardship and sadness in her words. I was emotionally overcome by this page and put the book back inside my coat for safekeeping. Sarah and I napped for a while and then awoke to an increasingly lower water level. I got ready to try to make it to the car and Sarah instinctively led the way. As I walked in the knee-deep water, I searched the trees to find the pathway. We made our way in the right direction through the ice cold water. After a long while of moving slowly through the water with Sarah swimming beside me, I finally saw the roof of the car. I hoped for the best as we drew closer. "At least the car's still there," I said to Sarah with some humor.

In silence, I worried about whether it would start. As I lifted the hood and took off my shirt to dry off the spark plugs, I whispered to myself, "Let it start . . . please let it start." It did.

Woo! I never felt this lucky before. I drove us out of the shadow of the mountain and counted my blessings along the way. I wanted to read more of the diary, but that would have to wait until I got us home safely.

CHAPTER FIVE

After returning home and immediately explaining to Meredith what had happened, I showed her what I had found. The only thing Meredith said was, "Wow, wow!" A hot bath sure did help my aching muscles and gave me time to read on.

The mountain flowers are so beautiful this time of year. There is a slight breeze in the tops of the trees. It is April or May now, I think. We were fortunate that our men returned with food for us a few weeks ago and our future looks brighter now. We have just planted corn in the big pasture south of here and are hoping for a pleasant summer. My son, Maiku, is growing fast and showing signs he will become strong like his father. I can see the pride in Suu Tavaci's eyes when he looks upon him, and can feel it myself, too. He is already learning to ride a yearling pony.

I do feel loneliness sometimes for my brother and sister back home, but the peace and happiness I feel here somewhat compensate. The settlers have been friendly of recent and come to trade with us occasionally. They like our moccasins and elk hide clothing. We make good use of the seeds that they bring us and the weapons for hunting. One of the traders from

Pueblo noticed the gold necklace I wear on special occasions. I was relieved when Suu Tavaci told him he had traded for it in the settlement, not wanting him to know that we had gold. The miners who come searching for the gold leave discouraged when we will not tell them where to find it. We have hidden all of the gold we could find. It is quite a lot. This place where we have put it should never be found by the treasure hunters. I will tell you, though, this special thing. You can find your treasure in the circle of life and death, and under the first moon. I will speak more of this to you. Please begin searching for my family.

I didn't know what her clues meant, but I was determined to begin my search for anyone related to Christiana. What did these clues mean about circles of life, death, and first moon? How was I going to get to the bottom of these clues? I had to read on to find out more. There were several pages left. I went directly to the next page.

Autumn leaves are falling now. This will be my ninth winter here. I am very worried. The traders brought a sickness to us. We have many people among us who are frightfully ill. We do have roots and natural medicines, but I am afraid the cure to this terrible thing cast upon us will take much more to cure. I am only one of the few among us who have not become ill. I think my life among the white people has given me resistance, but I am worried for Suu Tavaci and Maiku and Wacuwini Muatogoci, who is very sick now. I must gather more roots and fresh water now. I have been taught the medicinal uses of peyote plants, elk and bear root, and especially the yellow Unita Water Lilly which I gather from the little pond. This writing is important to me, but I must go now.

That was about the time Meredith came into the room and said,

"I think it's time now, Charlie." She had a serious look on her face. "Do you mean right now?" I said with surprise. "I think so," she replied. "I'll get our stuff." I started running around to get our pre-packed hospital bags and reached for my car keys. "Okay, I'm about ready." "Don't you think you should put some clothes on first?" Meredith asked with a big grin. "Oh yeah!" we laughed all the way to the hospital.

I pulled up to valet parking at the hospital and brought Meredith to the check-in counter. I was apprehensive as the necessary paperwork was painstakingly completed. I was embarrassed at the questions being asked of Meredith because they were so personal. "Call Cherrie," Meredith said with a definite attitude.

As I went to the pay phone to call Meredith's best friend Cherrie, I rehearsed in my mind the coaching lessons I'd received in the birth classes we'd gone to. After dialing Cherrie's pager, I remembered to call Meredith's mom and my mom, both of whom were as excited as I was. A nurse brought a wheelchair and took Meredith upstairs to her room, with me following behind and feeling totally out of control in the situation. As I turned on the television, I noticed the movie *Ziegfeld Follies* was on and realized it was one of Meredith's favorites. She watched as I assumed my coaching duties. "Not yet," the nurse said with a grin. "We still have time." Her grin turned to a laugh.

"Oh, I was just practicing," I exclaimed with embarrassment. "I think you've got it." She laughed

The movie was about over when Cherrie came into the room, explaining how she had been at the Pueblo Reservoir and came as soon as her beeper sounded. Nurses and doctors continued to come into the room in shorter intervals to take measurements and other things that I turned my head for. By midnight, another nurse came on duty and instructed Cherrie and I that it was time to go to work. We knew what that meant, and I was happy to have Cherrie there. As I went to Meredith's bedside, I noticed a glimmer of something pass by the doorway. Well, it wasn't just something, it was Christiana! No kidding. She sure gets around. She must have jumped in the car, I thought. By now, I was getting used to her and was glad to have her around.

My watch was ready, I was ready, and Cherrie and her ice chips were ready. As that same nurse gave a shot to Meredith for the pain, my heart filled with admiration for her and all women who go through this experience. As time went on and all of us grew weary, the nurse yelled to another, "Get the doctor!"

"I can't find the doctor," The other nurse replied with worry.

"No need to worry. I'm right here." The doctor stepped in.

In no time at all I was a proud father. Meredith had picked out a name, Mariah, which she had gotten from a song, "They Call the Wind Mariah," in the movie *Paint Your Wagon*. As Meredith's mom and dad entered the room, I felt a tremendous sense of relief that everything was okay. I knew Christiana was there to make sure as well. As I left for breakfast with Cherrie, I was still mystified by this miracle of an event. When I did calm down, I went home to read more of Christiana's diary.

CHAPTER SIX

I have come here today in much distress and great fear. A dear friend has confided in me of a conspiracy. There is much envy and jealousy of me by two squaws from another tribe who have come to live with us. Waini Agompi (Two Tongues) and her daughter, Atapii (Crow Feathers), have come from husband-less poverty and know not of the riches of a happy life. They wish to dispose of me and become the center of attention of this tribe. I feel deeply sad for them and their misguided desires. I have been told that murder would be no match for their desire for attention and power. I am a Ute now; however, they say my white skin is inferior and I have heard the whispers and seen their attempts to turn my friends against me. They know I can see through their mask now and with the warriors gone are planning to kill me by drowning. My friend Peini Togoiak (Three Thank You) has warned me just today. She has asked me to come to my secret place until a rider can return with Suu Tavaci. In spite of the threat to my life, I still feel compassion for ignorant souls of this sort. I do not think that they have enough heart and intelligence to know how wrong and small-minded they are. They put many decorations on their dwelling in times of celebration to be sure all notice them. Waini Agompi has

*acquired many feathers from willing braves and is sure to show them
off at all campfires. They often go out into the camp to tell of their
greatness with decorations, but the love of family has escaped them. I
think that— wait! I hear the sound of horses. It is Suu Tavaci. I am so
happy he wasn't far away. It is time for me to go with him.*

As I turned to the next page, I felt helpless that I hadn't been
there to help her.

*I have been spared from this threat and ugliness from my enemies.
Suu Tavaci has banished Waini Agampi and Atapii from our lands
forever. They have taken a warrior with them as he too wished for
wealth and power and was blinded by their persuasion. I shall not
mention his name because it was said he wished to kill Suu Travaci
and take his place as chief. They have gone now to rule over their own
tribe somewhere far away, I hope. I am much relieved now and must
return to prepare new moccasins for Suu Tavaci to wear on his ride to
catch up with his band of brave riders.*

The telephone was ringing and it was raining outside with
hail. Colorado hail storms come on quick and are quite a sight.
If you are indoors, that is. It was Uncle Johnny on the phone. "Is
that offer to visit still good?" he asked.

"Absolutely! I'd be glad to have your company," I responded.

Uncle Johnny had always been a favorite of mine. He had a
sense of humor that could keep you laughing day and night. His
lighthearted way of looking at the world was refreshing.

"Great, can we go to that gold panning spot your dad always
talked about?" he asked.

"Hell yeah, Uncle John! I'd like to have you with me when I

go back up to the mountains. When can you come to Colorado?"
I replied happily.

"I can come at the end of October, for two weeks," he said.

"That would be great. I'm going back up there to scout it out again soon before you get here and I'll have a fun surprise for you," I said with a tease.

"Ah, you're kidding me," he said with a laugh in the middle of his words. Uncle Johnny liked adventure. I remember him taking drives to New York with all who would go just for chili dogs.

"You're not going to get me lost in those big mountains, are you?" he asked.

"Not unless I'm with you," I chuckled.

"Should I bring a gun to protect us from mountain lions?" he snickered.

"Nah, Uncle John, that's okay. We'll have Sarah with us." I didn't mention my previous encounter with a mountain lion. "Bring some warm clothes because snow comes early in the mountains," I advised.

"Yah, I'll bring some high boots, too. In case you get a little carried away with your stories." He laughed as hard as he could.

As I hung up the phone, the doorbell rang. Glancing out the kitchen window, I saw Teddy, carrying a bundle of maps. Teddy is a good friend whom I had asked to get some maps of Park County and the surrounding region. I had known Teddy for many years and could confide in him any secret with trust. I'd told him all about Christiana and Dead Man's Gulch. "You aren't really going back up there after all that's happened, are you?" he asked, hoping for a negative reply.

"I have to go. I made a promise to myself to fulfill Christiana's wish. Also, I want to find that gold."

"You dummy, you could get killed!" he said, raising his eyebrows in concern.

"Nah, don't worry. I always seem to survive somehow." I wondered how long that luck would last.

"You want me to go with you? I'll bring my hook." Teddy had lost an arm in a motorcycle accident and had an artificial arm now to replace it.

"I might have use for your arm, Ted, but I'll have some tough climbing to do. I'm afraid you wouldn't want to try that. I'll save a gold nugget for you, though," I assured him.

"Okay, here are your maps. See you soon, and be careful, damn it," he grumbled.

After Teddy left, I opened the maps and studied them. I didn't have anything particular to look for, except I was wondering if I could get an overall picture of the watershed in that region. Gold nuggets, or what is called free gold, travel downstream in the shortest way because of their weight, which is about eight times heavier than water. Free gold, really isn't free; it's just free from the rock. The other way gold can be found is in ore deposits and veins. There are many gold ore deposits in the mountains of Colorado. But they are in different places than where free gold has been found.

The Cripple Creek area is famous for making many miners rich in the 1890s. However, I have not heard of anyone finding free gold in the stream below Cripple Creek in Phantom Canyon. In fact my dad, brothers, and I panned there several times without finding even a single gold flower. The ore has to be dug out of the ground, crushed, and processed with mercury. A ton of rock may yield just a single ounce of gold. People who have panned for gold in the Arkansas River, Clear Creek, or South Platte River have found nuggets weighing an ounce or much more. The Breckenridge and Alma area has yielded gold nuggets weighing many ounces. Cherry Creek was where gold was originally found in Colorado, and that began the first gold rush by hundreds of treasure hunters with wagons painted with *Pikes Peak or Bust!* on them.

While looking at those maps, I thought of another use for them. I charted my path for Meredith, for the next time Sarah and I went back up to Dead Man's Gulch—just in case we didn't come back in time. That trip would come soon, I hoped. First, I needed to finish reading the diary. Now I needed to pick up Meredith and little Mariah up at the hospital. Tomorrow was Sunday, so I'd have no distractions and could finish reading.

CHAPTER SEVEN

S unday morning came quickly. I was tired and slept very
well. Meredith didn't, however. She was awake often to
take care of Mariah. They were both asleep now. I took
the phone off the hook, made some coffee, and relaxed again in
my recliner with Christiana's diary. It was a foggy morning with
light rain. I turned on the reading light, pulled a blanket over my
cold feet, and turned the next page.

*This has been another hard winter. We were lucky the hunters had
a good trip to the Black Forest, which was plentiful with game. They
brought back deer and elk meat and hides, and stopped at a trading
post in Colorado City to trade for corn and flour. Three more traders
from Manitou Springs arrived today. They, just as other traders in the
past, have asked about the place where the Germans found the big gold
strike. We always tell them it must have been over in the south Sierra
Madre mountains. We are always afraid we will be overwhelmed by
white settlers who would rush here and destroy our way of life if any
of this gold were found. We have searched wide and collected all the
gold we could find. I tell you again to look for the circle of life and
death. In my last writing I shall try to make a map for you. I hope you*

hear my plea for my descendant's sake, and you will tell them of my fate for my own sake.

I am truly a Nuciu (one of the people) now. I have strong bonds here and I am quite content with my fate. We have had some difficult days struggling for survival, we also had some wonderful times. Yesterday we had games of bravery, strength, and survival for the youngest of our braves. Maiku has done well. He always shines above the others and will surely make a great chief when his time comes. He has a way with the ponies as if he can speak to them and they listen. His favorite pony comes to him at his command. We are proud and get great joy from the smile of satisfaction on his face. I have been honored for my ability to cook and get much respect from all of the Nuciu for the deerskin coats I have crafted. My life has been good of late, although not at all what I expected when I came west with my brother Henry.

I was full of excitement to discover the west and build a future. I expected to start a family in the settlements and maybe own a ranch. My sister, Mary May, and her husband, John Paul Chapin, decided to stay in Connecticut to start their own family. I hope they are well. I know she must have worried about me all of these years or thought I was dead with our brother Henry. I do not even know if she knows about his death. I place wildflowers on Henry and our companions' graves sometimes. I do not know which grave is Henry's because other whites have buried them in the place they were killed. I was not allowed to go there at first. The other dead souls are Jim Briggs, Johnny Whitely, Moses Hatcher, Jeffrey Starr, and Thomas Buckley.

Henry dreamed of opening a settler's store in Fountain Valley. Our trip to this mountain was to find enough gold to open that store. Henry had worked hard in various jobs to get enough money saved for us to make this trip out west. He had saved $400 and I had accumulated $150 for us to come here. It was hard to leave our sister, but this was our dream. We traveled by wagon to Philadelphia and then on to St. Louis. It was a difficult trip. The rains were heavy and persistent. The bugs afterward were horrible and always in our face. The mud made the trip very slow in the wagon. The wheels kept getting stuck and the horses were overworked. We covered a distance of just a few miles on some days. We left Connecticut in March and did not reach Wichita, Kansas until June. We joined up with many other travelers there to make the trip safer.

It was late July before we reached the mountains of Colorado. We could see the top of Pikes Peak for seven days before we actually reached its base. Rattlesnakes were a problem along the way, scaring the horses and those among us who were walking. No person was bitten and we were thankful for that. The Indian hunting parties we passed along the way were curious and watched us from every vantage point. Jolly Holden, the leader of our wagons, told everyone not to show fear or weakness. It was comforting to know he had scouted with the earliest trappers and had quite a reputation for being a crack shot. The winds in Kansas were unbearable at times and we had to put patches over our horses' eyes to keep the sand out of them. When we reached the foothills of Pikes Peak, we stopped at the territorial office in Colorado City where there was much activity.

Settlers like us were arriving every day. Johnny and Thomas overheard a conversation at the livery stable about two men who had *found much gold in the mountains. It was said that they had found a full sack of gold in just a couple of weeks. As Johnny and Thomas told us and the others in our party about the gold one night, there was much excitement and talk about going up there into those awesome mountains to find our stake. The mountains looked scary and also inviting. The clouds would drift over them so softly. Yet, when the storms came they were swift and violent. Jim reckoned we had enough time left before the winter weather came to go up there and have a look-see. No one disagreed. Jeffrey questioned how we might figure out where to go. He said, "Those two fellows didn't tell anyone where to go and find their gold." Moses volunteered to go over to the tavern and ask around for any clues on where to go. Upon his return he told us many of the prospectors had been going up to a place where the South Platte River begins. Jim was the most traveled of our group and we all turned to him to guide us there.*

"I'll be glad to make this trip, but I'll tell you all right now that when I say it's time to go, we go. I won't be a'kiddin'." So we made the decision to go.

We spent the next day gathering supplies and the tools we were going to need. Henry and Thomas went by the livery stable before we left to talk with a man named David Potts. Henry had spoken with him when we arrived and reckoned he knew the territory pretty darn well. This man Potts had been a trapper in the mountains before he had broken a leg and had to come down. I didn't care for him though. He was a beastly man, dirty and always cussing. Thomas enticed him to draw a map in trade for a bottle of good whiskey.

We began our trip under a cloudless sky. The trip took six days.

The climb up and around Pikes Peak was treacherous and slow at times with rock slides and flash storms. We followed Potts directions and they seemed true and accurate. We met up with another party of travelers returning from a trip in the direction we were going to. They looked at our map and confirmed its accuracy. When we finally arrived at this place, the men showed great joy to see the beautiful river, waterfall and promising-looking rocks. Jim spotted some gold dust right away. Henry went to his book immediately and wrote the word "Eureka! The game we had seen along the way looked plentiful, so Charlie went with Moses to get our dinner. They returned quickly with a deer that they shot with ease. I learned many weeks later that it was the sound of that shot which had alerted the Utes to our presence. That event seemed like forever, but it wasn't really all that long ago now. I never feel scared anymore. The men met their deaths quickly and I have come to accept it. I must go now and prepare food for Suu Tavaci and Maiku.

CHAPTER EIGHT

As I went into the kitchen for another cup of coffee, I was thinking that there weren't many pages left to read. This scared me. There was so much more I needed to know. The fog was lifting outside of the bay window. The sun was peeking through the crab apple tree and the squirrels were coming out for their free morning peanuts as were the blue jays, little thieves that they are. I grabbed a handful, threw them out the door, and got back to my reading.

It has been two seasons since I have been able to come here as the Nuciu have taken me with them over the snow-covered mountains they call the Great Mother of Paa (Water). Suu Tavaci is preparing for the great invasion of the settlers and believes we will have to leave our land soon to seek refuge in a place the white men will not go. He says the Great Mother will make a good wall to stop their bullets. We have found a place such as this valley over that great wall in a place Suu Tavaci calls the Grand Junction, where the waters meet and are swift. There is a valley with many deer and elk. This place also has east-facing hillsides for protection from the weather and warmth from the winter sun. We have come back to this place I have called home and found a new life in to get the old and very young Nuciu whom need much help to make the long journey. It is early summer here now, and we will need much time to gather supplies and make carts for the weak among us. Maiku is grown now and is much tested in all of the warrior and hunting skills. He has just returned from a scouting trip with four of his followers. They speak of a great gathering of white man's wagons at the foot of the big pass. He has said to us, "They prepare for the great invasion of our land."

There is much to be done and I have such little time. I wonder who might find my diary. I plead with you again to tell of my fate and pass on my words to my ancestors. You can see the circle where you may find your gold from the place where two prairie dogs kiss. Look to the— wait, I hear gunshots! I must go. Goodbye, and remember me as Christiana Mamaci Paa Fitsimmonds.

Oh no! What happened, I wondered. How exasperating this was. She didn't finish her sentence. What was her fate and that of the Nuciu? I wanted to find the hidden gold, but it seemed more important now to find out what happened to them and find any ancestor she might have. What did she mean about the place of kissing prairie dogs? Look to the what? Were they all killed or did they survive? I had just realized how much research I had in front of me and another trip to Dead Man's Gulch with Sarah.

I spent the rest of that day while Meredith cared for Mariah re-reading the diary and wondering what happened to Mamaci Paa.

That night I stayed awake for hours hoping to get a glimpse of Christiana again, or at least get a sign from her. I walked the house in the dark and sat quietly in my recliner. I tried talking to her and concentrated as hard as I could to no avail; there was no sign of her presence. I resigned myself to the realization that if I was to see her again it would be at a time of her choosing. My work was laid out for me. Was it ever! Now I had to use all of my imagination and skills to capture the lost history, find the lost people, and find that gold.

CHAPTER NINE

For the next several days there was much going on in my life and so much on my mind that I seemed to have a brain block. I just couldn't go forward in any direction at all, much less the right one. The harder I tried to think of the next step, the more frustrated I became. I didn't do well at my job. Being a salesman was the last thing I wanted to do. There were many more new chores around the house now with a new baby in the house. Meredith was exhausted from all she had been through and I began doing most of the dinner cooking. Sarah wasn't getting any attention and became very restless. I decided to take her for a ride to clear my mind of everything. Putting some oldies on the car radio always seemed to be a special tonic for me and eased my mind. We drove up to the foothills to a place called Seven Falls. Yes, another waterfall. This place is referred to as the grandest mile of scenery in Colorado and it sure must be. While Sarah and I were relaxing in the shade, I could hear the conversation of a newlywed couple sitting close by. "Davy, isn't this the prettiest place you have ever been to in your life?" The pretty red haired woman asked her man.

"It sure is, Marie. We must come back here for every one of our anniversaries." He smiled.

The melody of the water pulsing onto the rocks reminded me of Christiana. There was a minute when I could actually put myself at that spot sitting next to Mamaci Paa and trading stories. Sarah and I drove home as I hoped the next event would come soon. I wanted to go back to Dead Man's Gulch that next weekend. Shopping with Meredith for the new baby would make that option impossible. When I woke up Saturday morning, something seemed out of place to me. I made coffee and started looking around with just one eye open since the other hadn't woke up yet. Where are they when you need them? I knew something was out of place, but sure couldn't tell what it was. That is, until I sat in my recliner. I realized I was sitting on yesterday's newspaper. We never put it there. It always goes out to the recycle bin. Now I had to wonder: did I put it there while I was doing something else? I can remember so much, except sometimes I wonder what I went to the pantry for or what did I want in the refrigerator. Was this a message from Christiana? I chose to believe the message answer and immediately started wondering what the message was. I had read the paper the day before and couldn't think of anything of significance. I went through it again just to make sure. No, there was nothing there. Or was there? That's when it hit me! I remembered my history research training. I could look up events in the local newspaper on microfiche at the library. Some kind and dedicated people had cataloged the newspaper articles by name, events, and places and separated them by dates in a card catalog. I had a few free hours that day, so I went to the Penrose Library as soon as it opened.

When I arrived at the library with my notepad and lucky pen I went directly to the local history section and started looking through the card catalogs for names in articles. I doubted Mamaci Paa would be included, so I looked for Wacuwini Muatagoci since he had been the chief. I found one article in less than ten minutes. The article was titled "Ute chief dies! Contagious virus is the culprit." The card told me the page and paragraph of the article as well as the date of November 4, 1869. I looked up the right microfiche, loaded it on the machine, and went to the page. It was hard to read, as some microfiche are. I could see it well enough to read "Tom Nance, a trader with the Fountain Colony Trading Company, reports today that the chief of the Ute Indian Tribe has succumbed to the virus recently suffered by many in his group. His son, Suu Tavaci, is now chief of the Ute Indian tribe in Park County."

That was it, no more. It was a small success for me to know I could get more information. Next, I searched for Suu Tavaci, but the catalog referenced the same article. Then I searched for articles about Maiku. I found one article and went back to the microfiche. It read "A new land grant and treaty has been signed yesterday between Maiku, the chief of the Ute Indians, and the commissioner from the Federal Bureau of Indian Affairs. Details of the pact are not available at this time." Well, at least he survived the events of the day I was looking for, I thought.

I decided to skip directly to events and search, wanting to find out what happened the day of Christiana's last diary entry. She wanted to be remembered as Christiana Mamaci Paa Fitsimmonds, but to me she was still Christiana. First, I searched for Indian wars thinking there could have been one that day. There were many articles with this topic, but none referred to this time or the Ute's. Next, I tried looking for "skirmish," thinking it might not have been a big deal to the local newspaper. There were many articles in this category, but I got lucky. I saw the title "Skirmish reported in Park County with Indians." That might be it. I went right to it. It read "Jesse Yance rode into town today from Park County. He was an advance scout for the Fishman settlers group heading in that direction to settle new lands. Jesse and a group of four other scouts came upon a group of Indians near the place known as Dead Man's Gulch. Not knowing if these Indians were friendly, one of the other scouts hastily drew his pistol and began firing at them. A skirmish broke out and three of the scouts were wounded, as was one of the now-hostile Indians. The scouts were wise to withdraw as they spotted a much larger party of Indians on their way out of the gulch."

Okay, I thought, Mamaci Paa got away safely. Now I relaxed a little, knowing more of what had happened. I drove home thinking about my next plan.

CHAPTER TEN

Knowing I had so much research to do kept my mind busy. This next Saturday was just for fun. Sarah and I were getting ready to go back to Dead Man's Gulch. I was packing and she was sitting next to the door waiting for me. She was perceptive and seemed to know what was coming based on what I was doing. As soon as she saw my backpack come out she whined and jumped up at the door. We had permission from Meredith to go and she had a map of where we were going. The weather was nice and the weatherman, who was never wrong,—well, lets say he was right once in a while—was saying there were no storms in the forecast. Of course, we were going up into the mountains where there is no such thing as a weather forecast. I packed lots of treats for Sarah and extra sandwiches this time for me.

As we were walking out the door, Meredith was in the hallway holding Mariah to say goodbye. Our three cats sat in a line wondering what these people they thought they owned were up to now. There was Annabel, the little princess who was too uppity to give a darn about anything other than her next nap. Then there was Milkbox, who was waiting for his chance to escape out of the front door and go carousing. I had to rescue him from the roof of the neighbor's house a few years before and let him stay on our porch. He began sleeping in the milk box before we brought him into his kingdom. There was also crazy little Bobo (Bodangles). Meredith gave her that name because she was rescued from an encounter with a cedar fence on which she hung on and stuck for about a day. I guess we were just an extension of the animal rescue society. Sarah was also rescued from the Great Pyrenees Rescue Society. Meredith and I had been walking downtown in Colorado Springs when we saw her sitting next to a nice lady at an outdoor café. In my kidding nature I said, "Oh what a pretty dog, may I have her?"

"Well, if you have a big enough house you can. That's why I'm here, to get her adopted out. You see, I rescue Great Pyrenees dogs and currently have thirteen to give away," the happy lady replied.

"Okay, we'll take her," I said, confirming my delight. Well, that was that. We got Sarah and now she has rescued me from a mountain lion.

Heading toward the pass, now called the Ute Pass, I could see the Garden of The Gods in the distance and was thinking of Wacuwini Muatagoci and his final send-off. I was more inclined to be thinking of the clues given to me by Christiana and where or if I could find that gold. I didn't understand about the circle of life and death or the first moon, so I thought I would try to find this place of kissing prairie dogs. I reasoned that it must have been an outstanding feature of the countryside. Could it have been an unusual tree, hillside, rock, or a part of a stream? That was part of the fun of it. I love mysteries.

We arrived at Green Mountain Falls; a quaint little town located up the Ute pass. I decided to stop off for breakfast at a favorite restaurant. It was a little log hut that served up the best green chile breakfast burrito I'd ever eaten. Sarah liked to wade in her favorite little pond next to the Gazebo. In a hurry now to get going, I left the restaurant, called for Sarah, and drove back up the pass to see what was waiting for us. It was a beautiful summer day with a slight cooling breeze and a few clouds in the sky. We drove up and through them going by Woodland Park. Yes, the mountain is that high—over 14,000 feet in altitude! Previously, on a winter's day, we'd driven up and out of a snowstorm. Who would have thought that was possible? There was no snow this day though, just blue skies and clear sailing—so far at least.

As I passed a town named Deckers and drove alongside the South Platte River, my thoughts turned to a more serious nature. I was thinking about gold now. Next to the river was a long pasture where we could see elk grazing. This field was what is called a glacial moraine, which is formed by ice glaciers a long time ago. The pressure of the ground movement creates upturned mounds. These are likely places to find gold. In fact, many a gold hunter had picked up a good day's pay in that area. A good day's pay in the late 1800s was considered to be about $1.50, which was about the average for that area and along Clear Creek and Cherry Creek.

In my continuing education, which started with my dad's membership in The Gold Panning Association, I had learned that this was actually the third set of Rocky Mountains. The first mountains formed billions of years ago and at one time the region was covered in water. All three sets of mountains were formed by movements in the earth's plates before dinosaurs were roaming this region. The area which is now called the Front Range along the east side of the mountains, including Colorado Springs and Denver, was also a rainforest at a time long ago.

When the mountains sprang up, they prevented the long rainy days and the weather changed to provide whatever moisture the clouds could drop in closely to the foothills. I'm not a meteorologist, but I did believe the movie I watched at a local tourist visitor's center. There are remains of dinosaur beds in a little town called Florissant, which was a place of many good dinosaur bone finds. It has been said that turquoise was plentiful in that region. I learned in my research that there was an Indian village along Rampart Range Road that produced a lot of jewelry. I made several trips there without finding it. The Ute Indians were quite adept at making jewelry and used much turquoise for that purpose.

I was thinking about all I had learned with my dad about gold and where it might be. An old hunter and part-time geologist told us gold can sometimes come out of the ground in white quartz. I thought I'd pay more attention for this rock when I got to Dead Man's Gulch. The region this gulch was in and over the mountain valley to Breckenridge and Alma had produced the largest gold nuggets in the state. The largest gold nugget recorded, eleven ounces, was found there. Gerry, our gold hunter friend explained to us how gold traveled down the rivers after coming out of the ground.

Gold, which is eight times heavier than water, takes the shortest path because of its weight. When it gets behind boulders in the river, it will sink to the bottom to bedrock. Because of floods and the existence of ancient stream beds, gold can be found where there is no water at all now. It also can be found on a hillside where it has come out of the ground after a spring thaw has broken apart the rock in which it was contained.

In rivers, gold is usually found in or around black sand. This black sand is finely ground up rock and is very heavy. With a magnifying glass you can see the full spectrum of colors and particles that include rubies, diamonds, garnets, turquoise, and others. What I thought I was looking for, though, might be gold nuggets—great big gold nuggets. What a nice dream!

I had been dreaming so much that I suddenly arrived at Dead Man's Gulch in what seemed like just a few minutes. Sarah was barking now. She wanted out of the car and I was ready to go, too.

CHAPTER ELEVEN

As we drove through the shady grove of pine trees, with the river rushing quickly by, a mule deer stepped out in front of us. It was a good-sized buck with several antlers grown over with moss. He looked at us curiously and bolted across the dirt road into the trees. I thought this must be a good sign. Better than a grizzly bear or that short-tempered mountain lion! At the same spot in the road we had previously parked, I pulled over and let Sarah out of the back of the Jeep. While grabbing my back pack, Sarah growled. This was not like her. I looked around and spotted two men approaching us. My first thought was that if Sarah doesn't trust them, then I shouldn't either. Sarah liked people and was almost always friendly. I was sure her instincts must be for a reason.

"Good morning, stranger," were the first words from the man with the red bandana tied around his forehead.

"Good morning," I replied.

"Are you looking for something up here?" The second man asked as he stepped away from Sarah. He was large and sassy and totally devoid of charisma.

Thinking quickly, I spotted the fishing pole in the back of the Jeep that I always brought along on trips.

"Well yes, I am looking for a big rainbow trout." I went to grab my pole and bait box from the back of the Jeep.

The gruff guy tried and succeeded poorly in blurting out a chuckle. "We thought you might be here looking for gold or something."

Chuckling back, I said, "Everybody knows there's no gold left up here."

The man with the bandana asked, "What do you mean? Isn't this Dead Man's Gulch?"

"Sure," I said. "Everyone knows those two German guys in the 1800s took out all of the gold that could be found here." I knew the gold nuggets left here were hidden and may not have been found yet.

I sensed these two men were testing me and were here to get gold for themselves. They wanted to see if I was their adversary in that search. I instinctively said, "The only thing to be found here now is those big trout in the river."

"Oh," said the first man. "Well, we sure do wish you luck." They backed away from Sarah, then turned and slithered away like the snakes Sarah and I both thought they were.

Alarms went off in my head—big alarms! I didn't think these tough guys would be too aggressive as long as Sarah was by my side, but I knew that they had it in them if the occasion presented itself. For now I was content to take my fishing gear down to the river. All the while I hoped they didn't find any of the gold dust that my dad and I had once discovered. If they knew there really was gold there, they surely wouldn't give up. So much for the lucky mule deer, I thought to myself.

I found a comfortable spot to sit under a scrub oak tree next to the west bank on the river. I decided to make the most of my day. Sarah stayed close to my side as I grabbed some treats for her out of my backpack. Rummaging through my tackle bag I found a Pistol Pete fly that I had been hoping for a chance to try ever since I heard an acquaintance bragging about how many fish he had caught down on the Arkansas River. I sure didn't believe he had caught that many, but I thought it was worth a try. I tied it onto my line, threw it in, set my pole on a rock, and glanced away from it to see where those two characters were going. I could see them occasionally in between the rock slopes going up the mountain side. When I looked back I could see my fishing pole bobbing up and down and from side to side. I was surprised and startled by the good action at the end of the pole. Picking it up, I realized what a good fight I had on my hands. Sarah started barking. She knew what was going to happen. Sarah had been on fishing trips with me before. The fish fought its way back behind a big boulder in the river, got some slack in the line and, just like that, was off. I could hear a big whale of a laugh from mister gruff up on the hillside. He was obviously keeping an eye on me. I was content with that result. I didn't need dinner that day. Well, I didn't think I was going to need dinner. Sarah and I relaxed for a while again.

I was definitely feeling like I should leave and come back on a safer day. I couldn't. This mission I was on had become way too important to me. I decided to watch these guys for a while to see if they found anything, but I would head for the car if they started coming my way again. Two o'clock clouds started rolling in now. That is so typical in Colorado, especially in the mountains. Sarah lifted her head back up, sniffing into the air and looking downstream. In another minute I could see a fox slipping through the brush to get a drink of water. The little chickadees were jumping from one tree branch to another and singing to each other. Those two guys seemed to be huddled together now as if they were talking something over. On occasion they glanced my way. I looked away so as not to stare at them and tried to be nonchalant. When I thought it was okay to look back, they were gone. Several minutes went by without seeing either one of them. I was starting to think that the coast was clear.

That was about the time I heard a scary noise behind me. *Click!* It was the sound of a gun hammer being pulled back. I had heard that noise before, but this was the first time it had sounded threatening to me. "Hold on to that damn dog, and you had better not move or I'll shoot you both," mister gruff said.

"Ah shit. Sarah, stay girl."

"We're going to need to borrow your car, stranger," mister bandana said in a rather shaky voice.

"Now I'll tell you what you're going to do and we might leave you tied up here without killing you. Firstly, I'm going to toss this rope to you and you're going to tie that damn growling dog up to that tree stump next to you. Got it?"

"Yes I got it," I responded in a matter-of-fact manner.

"Okay then, here you go." He threw a piece of rope to me. I held Sarah with one hand, knowing she would go after them if she could, and caught the rope with the other.

"Now tie up that damn dog or I just might shoot you because I like killing!"

Without a word, I tied one end of the rope to Sarah's collar and the other end to the tree stump. She looked at me and whined a little. I hugged her and said, "It's okay, girl. Okay."

"Now, you toss over those god damn car keys of yours," mister gruff continued.

I reached into my left front pocket and complied with his demand.

"This must be your lucky day because Louis hasn't shot you yet," mister bandana said.

"Tie his ass up to that other tree stump over yonder," mister gruff responded with voice ripe with mean satisfaction.

The big man came toward me. Sarah growled and tried to free herself. He grabbed me hard and pushed backward toward the tree stump. I wanted to punch mister gruff. I had been a pretty good fighter when I was young. I had never fought with a man with a gun, though. I had Sarah to worry about and Meredith with a new baby at home. After he thoroughly tied me up, they both stepped away a few feet and whispered to each other. The whispering stopped and I closed my eyes. I was thinking they might shoot us anyway. I wondered if this was going to be the first bucket of you-know-what I wouldn't get out of.

That's when I felt the gun barrel push into my side. "We're

taking your goddamned money too, stranger," mister gruff said.

"Get his wallet too; it might have some credit cards," mister bandana told him.

As he took my wallet, mister gruff asked me, "Got anything else on you?"

"No I don't." Sarah was going crazy now, jumping and twisting, trying to get loose.

"Calm down that damn dog or I'll do it with a bullet to the head," mister gruff said.

"This might by your lucky day. We aren't going kill you yet. Don't try anything or I'll tell Louis to go ahead and shoot you." They walked toward the car laughing. "How much money did we get Louis?" mister bandana asked.

"There's over three hundred bucks here, Jester," mister gruff replied.

They got into the Jeep in very good spirits. I watched them drive away with my car, wallet, and money, leaving me and Sarah tied up in a precarious way.

I looked up at the ever-darkening sky and knew what was coming next. "This might not be a very good day." Sarah cried to me. "Can you chew through that rope, girl?" Sarah was smart, but I didn't think she could understand that much English. She was trying to pull the rope loose, but it wasn't going to give way. That's when the rain started coming down. I cringed when the big drops began hitting us faster and faster. *Please don't hail* I was thinking. "Ah crap! Here comes the hail; it's definitely not a good day." We were both being pelted. I had seen bigger hail than that in Colorado, but never at a time when I couldn't get away from it. Damn it hurt. Luckily, the hail was short-lived and we sat there all tied up, getting soaked. We were alive, though, and I kept an optimistic attitude, even laughing at the predicament at times. Sarah lay there looking over at me with big brown eyes. When the rain finally did subside the birds came back out and so did a pair of black squirrels. That was a good sign the weather would clear. I knew the animals always seemed to know what the weather was going to do. We were drenched, but there was still time for the sun to come out and dry us before the dark of night came. I closed my eyes for a while and tried to think of some way to escape and fell asleep.

As I dreamed—what I could remember from it—I saw an enormous fire on the other side of the river where Sarah and I were tied up. The wicciups behind the fire were many and disappeared into the darkness. Many squaws huddled and prepared a feast. Warriors danced to the beat of merry drums. Chiefs with feathers of plenty sat and smoked pipes to the rhythm of slow-moving flames. Wolf eyes lingered in the darkness behind a tree grove. They were watching me and thinking of their own feast. Then I saw an even more terrifying creature.

Awakening in a start, I had been thinking about that mountain lion we had encountered in our previous trip. If he came back around now, we would be in big trouble. There was no slack at all in the rope tying my hands behind the tree stump. I could barely move and the stump had a live branch off to one side preventing the rope from moving. I couldn't just stand up and slip away. Sarah's rope had about a foot of slack in it. She wouldn't be able to do much to fight the big cat this time. "Stop it," I said out loud to myself. "Don't worry about things you can't do anything about." Sarah looked over, thinking that I was talking to her. As I thought about more pleasant things, I realized that Meredith had the map I gave her. I was thinking if we could survive the night, help would come. As the sun started to dry and warm us, I thought about the trout for dinner. I was quite sure he wouldn't jump out and offer himself up to us, and he didn't, either.

As the darkness settled in, I was grateful for the clear Colorado sky. I could see many stars now that I was so high up in the mountains with the aid of a near full moon. The little light they provided us was reassuring. I somehow fell back into a deep sleep. When I awoke to the sound of an owl hooting, I was surprised to see Sarah sitting next to me. She had chewed through the rope tied to her while I was asleep. "Good girl, Sarah, good girl," I said with a happy pet on her head.

I went back to sleep then, knowing she could protect me now from that mountain lion or whatever might come around us. There were big bears up there, too.

In the morning I awoke glad to be safe, but sore from that uncomfortable position. I felt sure Meredith had called someone to come and find us. I tried to get Sarah barking so anyone looking for us could hear her. "Make some noise, Sarah." She responded as loudly as I had ever heard and kept barking for well over a half hour. That was when I spotted the top of a pickup truck coming up the cart path. It was white with a yellow bubble on top. A forest ranger, I thought. Yep, it sure was! The tall man got out of his truck and walked quickly toward us. He was like the lone ranger to me this day. He carried a holster with a big iron on his hip and smiled with confidence saying, "Good morning, you seem to have a little problem."

Sarah jumped up and licked his face, knowing he was a good guy. "Well, I can't remember when I've had a bigger problem. I sure am grateful that you are here."

"I heard your dog barking. We got a call from the state police to come up here and look for you two. Your wife called them about midnight and gave us directions. It was a good thing for you that she had that map you drew or you might be here for a very long time."

"Yah, it sure is." I was relieved.

"How did you get all tied up like this?"

I told him the story about those two snakes.

"Oh. We've been looking for those two criminals." He untied me, ran back over to his truck, and started talking on his radio.

I stood up and stretched my sore muscles, then walked over to the stream and splashed cold water on my face. The ranger was still talking on his radio, so I walked over to my backpack and grabbed one of those bottles of beer. Taking a big swig, I said to Sarah, "Damn, that's good. Looks like we're saved, girl." She barked once in agreement and I gave her the last couple of sips.

The ranger came back over to me. "My office is going to call your wife and let her know you two are safe. Can you describe those two guys?"

I gave him a description of them both and told him that I heard them call each other Louis and Jester.

"We know who they are. The police have been looking for them for three weeks. They escaped from the federal prison in Canon City. You are very fortunate because they are big-time criminals. They were both in prison for kidnapping and manslaughter. Let's get you two out of here. I'll get your gear. What is your dog's name?"

"Sarah."

"Well, hello Sarah." He reached down to pet her.

We got into the truck and rode out of the gulch when he turned on the radio and asked for an all points bulletin on my Jeep. I asked him to have someone call Meredith and ask her to have someone meet me at the Kathy's Hotel in Woodland Park. The ranger, Myron Garrison was his name, sure did save the day. He reassured me it wouldn't be too long before the state police found those guys and my Jeep. He dropped us off at the hotel and went off to join the hunt.

I took Sarah into the restaurant for breakfast before I realized I didn't have any money. I asked for Kathy, whom I had known for many years, but she wasn't in at the moment. I was disappointed because I really did want to see her. If you knew Kathy, you would always want her company. She was always nurturing and thoughtful. Standing there in the front of the restaurant, bewildered and searching my pockets, someone behind me said, "Need some breakfast money?" Turning, I saw the ranger. He had turned around after realizing my money had been stolen.

"Sure could," I said in relief. "I can mail it back to you."

"No worries, I've been in that spot before." He chuckled and walked away. I wondered what he meant by that. Had he been robbed at some time in his life? I thought maybe that's why he became a ranger.

Sitting down with Sarah next to me, I ordered the biggest breakfast on the menu and one for Sarah, too. That was one terrific breakfast. We went to a comfy chair on the front porch to wait for a ride home. I didn't have to wonder who was coming for very long. My good friend Teddy showed up out front with a big smile on his face. "You need me to rescue you?"

"You had better rescue me," I said with a laugh, "or Meredith might be a little unhappy with you."

"Oh no, I don't want that. Let's go, treasure hunter." He laughed "I have a new nickname for you, Charlie. It's the captured treasure hunter."

It was a long ride home wondering what Meredith was going to say. She hugged us both and said she was just glad we were safe. I got a phone call from that ranger the next day. He said they caught the two criminals near Raton, New Mexico and I could pick up the Jeep there at the state police barracks when I wanted to. Teddy drove me down there the following Saturday and I was happily surprised to see it undamaged. "Looks like I found some more of those roses my dad always talked about," I said to Teddy.

"Yah, I guess so. I sure wish you would quit pushing your luck," he replied.

I didn't say anything, but I was thinking, *Yah, me too.*

CHAPTER TWELVE

I promised Meredith I wouldn't go back up there for a while, but I was sure that I could go when Uncle Johnny arrived. I could be content with adventurous trips to the library to do some more research for the time being. On my way out the door for one of my research trips, I found a check in the mailbox. It was from the Department of Corrections in the amount of $5,000. The letter said the check was for my assistance in the apprehension of those criminals, Louis and Jess. How nice! Meredith might change her mind about my trips to the gulch now, I hoped.

When I got to the library, I decided to read old newspapers on the microfiche to see what I might find. That was so interesting; everyone should do it. It gave me an interesting viewpoint of reality in the 1800s. I learned much from those articles about the people who were the pioneers of Colorado Springs.

Christiana was already one of the Nuciu when General Palmer and his Colorado Springs Company incorporated Colorado Springs in 1871. He had purchased the land from the Philadelphia Company and through the years had donated much of it for schools and other public needs. He was a charitable man and certainly deserves the statue of him on his horse downtown. There were other people who contributed much to the survival of the town. Tom Brigham was one of those pioneers. He was the first cattleman in town and opened the first butcher shops. He helped feed the townspeople, miners going up to Leadville, and whatever persons he could help with meal donations. Widows were always a recipient of his donations. Many people from the east with tuberculosis came to the region for its dry climate. Colorado College was opened and is now one of the highest rated colleges in the country. Famous people of the time would travel here and give speeches. Teddy Roosevelt and other presidents have given speeches in the town at the foot of Pikes Peak. P.T. Barnum gave a talk at the little city building once called Unity Chapel.

Volunteer firemen used horses and wagons to go to fires. The local dairy farmer would milk his cows twice a day so everyone had fresh milk. The kids attended school in little wooden buildings called annexes. Large building lots could be purchased for $200—$10 down and payments of $5 a month with 12 percent interest. Some people got chattel mortgages with horses and wagons as collateral. People were trading in little wooden stores and their customers began having lots more money to spend in the 1890s when gold was found in Cripple Creek. That wasn't my gold, though. So I decided to take a trip to the Denver Library to try to find more about the Utes, Mamaci Paa, and her family. I wondered all of the time what had happened to her. She obviously didn't return for her diary and gold necklace, so I assumed she spent the rest of her days on the western slope.

That is where I found the first clue and much, much more. I had been told by one of the staff at the library that many archives had been sent there because it was the capitol of the state. I immediately started looking at the files of the Denver newspaper of the time. I was lucky enough to find an article about Maiku. The article was titled "Ute Indian chief marries French woman serving as Indian translator from Glens Falls, New York, at Garden of the Gods." The date was August 12, 1888. The article went on to say that Maiku had wed Mary Rivet in a public ceremony with much celebration and Indian Sun dances. Now I had a possible last name for any children who may have come from that marriage. How funny, I thought. That is where my dad was born. Just a coincidence, I was sure. The article finished by saying the ceremony was held near the burial site of his grandfather, Wacuwini Muatogi, his father, Suu Tavaci, and his mother, Mamaci Paa. I knew she had died, but this was proof of where she was. I was saddened by this, yet happy for her that she received the proper burial and she didn't die violently in some forgotten canyon. On my way home that day, I tried to develop a strategy to find the children, if any, and I knew just how to do it. I would go back to the library and follow any obituaries I could find. I knew I needed one or two more trips to the Denver public library. I was also determined to find whatever information I could about the Ute Indians.

On my way home that day, I was so deep in thought I didn't

realize a dangerous moment in my life was just about to spring itself upon me. Early October in Colorado can bring sudden snow, especially in the higher elevations. I had just passed through a town called Castle Rock when the snow began to fall. I didn't think much of it because I had made that trip in snow so many times. There was heavy truck traffic that afternoon and I was driving in the fast lane around the trucks, still thinking about Christiana. A few miles up, at a town called Larkspur, on a short corner, I suddenly saw a dead deer in the road in front of me. With a tractor trailer to my right and no escape, I readied myself for a big bump. I was traveling at 70 mph when my car hit the dead deer. I received not only a bump, but a blown tire from the antler, which I didn't expect. My car went off the highway in a hurry and in between the guard rails, nearly rolling over. I had slowed down just enough after hearing a faint whisper in my ear, *Danger!* I wondered if this was a coincidence. Maybe; maybe not. I made it home safe again. I wondered how many times I could keep doing that in the face of continuing and unexpected danger.

Life was much less dangerous at the Colorado College library the following weekend. I stopped there on the way to the city library to have a look at the archives pertaining to the Ute Indian tribe. I was lucky enough to find a real bonanza of information and learned much about them and their customs. They believed they were descended from the bear. One of their springtime dances was called the bear dance. The sun dance was reserved for special celebrations such as the wedding ceremony for Maiku and Mary Rivet. The shelters originally used by them were called

Wicciups. They were made using tree bark; however, they began using teepees for the sake of easier movement. They took several wives, just as the Mormons did. They lived in forests and used deer and other animal hides for clothing. They finally moved to the western slope of Colorado and owned over one million acres of land in Utah. Before I left, though, a headline caught my attention. "Missing woman not among dead at massacre in Park County." It read: *A trader of goods just back from Park County reported that a white woman lives among the Ute Tribe. Daniel Beck reports that he believes this woman, whom the Utes call Mamaci Paa, to be a survivor of the party massacred at Dead Man's Gulch some years ago. Chief Suu Tavaci would not allow Beck to talk with the woman. However, on his way from the Ute camp he reported meeting two squaws who talked about her. They told him this woman was found after the massacre and was protected by Suu Tavaci. She wears an honored feather of the chiefs in her hat. If this report is true, the real name of this white woman living among them is not known.*

Well, I knew who she was. I was becoming more confident as I put together all of the pieces. I didn't have as good of luck finding the obituaries I needed that day or in the trips that followed back to Denver. I wasn't going to give up, no matter what.

The next evening was a good time to forget about my puzzle. Meredith's family came over to our house for a barbeque. We always enjoyed hosting parties for one of the nicest families I had ever met. There was Big, Louise, Gary, Randy, Marva, Meredith Dawn, and Rebecca. We also hosted James, Sean, Judy, James, Kelley, Shirley, and John. I relaxed by cooking some salmon and brisket on the smoker, which was one of my favorite things to do. We also invited Leah and Kelly, who I had met at the Colorado Springs Pioneers Museum. They were the most knowledgeable and helpful researchers I met and were genuinely nice people. The subject of my current research didn't come up that night. We all relaxed and had a good time.

Leah and Kelly invited me to the museum to learn about their tools for history research and were quite helpful during the journey that I was on. I certainly knew I needed all of the help I could get. I also stopped in at the El Paso County records office that week and met Diana. That smiling lady helped me to learn how to search old county records. I couldn't have imagined how many types of detailed records were kept back in the 1800s. As I was being educated, I became more and more fascinated by the sophistication of the early pioneers. This fact was not reflected in any old west movies I had seen. Reality can sometimes be far different than what we think it is. I was determined to be as stubborn as I needed in order to find Christiana's reality.

CHAPTER THIRTEEN

I was happy with my research progress by the time Uncle Johnny arrived that last Friday in October, and I was extremely happy to have some good company on another trip up to Dead Man's Gulch. I was content to have a favorite uncle with me in Colorado. I had never gotten over coming from such a big family and not having any relatives around me very often. Besides that, he brought a cooler full of Uncle Joe's great chili dogs with him. What a great guy. You should have seen the smile on his face when he handed that cooler to me at the airport. "You can't eat them all by yourself," he said. "I want some too." He always laughed and it was contagious. "Hey, what's that surprise you were talking about on the phone?" he asked.

"Lets stop on the way home and pick up some cold ones and I'll tell you all about that surprise." It was a good thing we picked up the cold ones because it took me until eleven that night to tell him all about Christiana and Dead Man's Gulch.

"You weren't kidding, were you? Holy cow, man, are you crazy or is this for real?" He was astonished.

"I'm not kidding about anything, Uncle Johnny. It's all real," I soberly responded.

"Man, what the hell were you thinking going up there by yourself and getting into those situations?"

"I wasn't alone. I had Sarah with me." I smiled.

"Yah, it's a damn good thing that your luck was with you that time. Your dad was right about you stepping in those buckets and coming out smelling like a rose every time. I hope our trip up there will be a lot less eventful." He laughed again.

Meredith was sitting in her comfy chair and rolled her eyes back. I'm sure she was thinking that wasn't likely. I'm glad she had a good sense of humor. That is about the time I went to my secret hiding place, of which I am not telling, and brought back the necklace and diary. I wish I had a picture of Uncle Johnny's face for that event. I don't think he went to sleep too quickly that night. He said he woke up a few times expecting to see Christiana.

The next morning, I made a terrific breakfast for everyone. It must have been, judging by the compliments. I can cook well, even if I do say so myself. Sarah loved Uncle Johnny and could not stop kissing him. That gave Uncle Johnny the giggles. It sure was contagious. The whole kitchen was giggling before breakfast was finished. Meredith was much more comfortable with the idea of Sarah and me going with some good company, especially a guy like Uncle Johnny who was good with his fists in the event any more bad guys showed up.

The weather forecast in the mountains called for possible snow showers. That was typical for late October. Of course, if any job was more difficult than being a weatherman in Colorado, I would not want it. It must be too difficult to predict what the clouds are going to do once they crash into the high mountain peaks. I have seen days where a blizzard was predicted and saw a dusting of snow and days when light snow was predicted and we got a blizzard. I really didn't think anything like that would happen on this trip. I made sure we both brought coats just in case. Sarah, of course, had her own coat.

I packed well for the trip; experience made me cautious. I brought extra sandwiches, Sarah food, water, and cold beer, which I never forgot! I brought lighted magnifying glasses for Uncle Johnny to check out all of the colors in the black sand and small plastic eye drop bottles to put in any gold dust we might find. I was planning on and hoping to find the lost treasure—hidden treasure, that is—but I wanted to be sure Uncle Johnny had some gold to take home with him. That was my first priority, to find some gold for him and then go for the big find. I had that in the back of my mind all of the way up the pass, even as I played tour guide. I explained all that I knew about Colorado to Uncle Johnny.

As we reached Woodland Park, the City above the clouds, he was awestruck at how we actually ascended through and above the clouds. "This is so darn cool," he said. When we reached Divide and could see as far as the Continental divide, he said, "That is the farthest I have ever been able to see. You have got to be kidding me!" His eyes were wide open. I had taken a different route to our destination this time for the scenery. I decided to stop off at the Tarryall Creek to pan a little and that was just fine with Uncle Johnny and Sarah, both of whom needed a rest break.

Getting out of the Jeep and scouting the river for black sand, I quickly found a good spot on the bank of a bend in the river. Scooping up some of the black sand in my little camp shovel, I handed the magnifying glass to Uncle Johnny and asked him to have a look. His look was that of puzzlement, asking, "How is it possible to see so many colors in sand that appears so black with the naked eye?"

"Life is full of tricks I think, Uncle Johnny. That is one of them." I looked over at his grin.

He laughed and said, "You ass, you really avoided that question pretty well."

Laughing back, I said, "Well, I guess old Jerry told me that black sand is actually what all of the colors look like when they are all together."

"That's better. Now you're smartening up." He laughed as hard as he could and continued, "You probably just made that up, didn't you?"

We panned out a couple of pans full of good dirt and didn't find any dust. "Well, let's get going to where the real gold is."

"Was this practice for rookies?" he snarled.

"Well yah! When we get to the good place, you'll want to know what you're doing, won't you?" I escaped my predicament as a pretend teacher.

"Sure, Charlie. You crack me up." He laughed. We got in the car and headed for my secret place in the sky.

I had to tell Uncle Johnny about my first gold panning trip with Dad and my brother Donnie. We went to Phantom Canyon that first day, thinking that there must be gold there because the river flowing through it came down the mountain from Cripple Creek and Victor, which were both famous for its rich gold mines. Donnie was naturally funny without even trying. The legacy he left behind was all laughs. His untimely death haunted me. "It was a rainy day when we set up a campfire next to the river behind that mountain." I pointed to the southeast. "Donnie was in the river before we could get the coolers out of the car. His third pan full of bottom dirt yielded a BB, of all things. What were the chances of finding a BB in the river if you were looking for one? Donnie was very excited at first, thinking the shiny ball could have been a nugget."

Uncle Johnny chuckled. "Only Donnie could have found that."

"Yah, if he didn't have bad luck, he had no luck," I said with admiration for the brother I had loved and protected at times.

"He sure was rich in his outlook on life."

I told him we didn't find any gold because there was none in the river. We didn't know the difference at the time between free gold and gold ore. There was another trip I told of with my brother Roger and his wife Carol, sons RJ and Rich, and daughter Kelly. We went up to the Arkansas that day near a town called Granite. We worked hard that day with a sluice box and panned out lots of sand. We did find a few gold flowers that day and everyone was happy for the experience. Roger is the kind of guy who was all grown up by the time he was twelve—and I'm not kidding. It takes a lot to get him excited. Carol is so mellow that she goes along with whatever Roger wants to do. They're both pleasures to be with. Their sons and daughter are the best nephews and niece a guy could ask for. I decided to make sure they got some of the treasure from Dead Man's Gulch if I could find it.

Of course, I had to tell him about the time my mom and her friend Gerry went with me up to the mountains. We filled up a couple of trash cans full of black sand from Clear Creek and brought it home to set up the sluice box for Gerry to sift through. I'll be damned if he didn't get a small gold nugget out of those two barrels' worth of sand. "What were the odds of that, Uncle Johnny?" I asked.

"With you, pretty good," he said with an all-knowing chuckle only he seemed to have.

Mom was funny that day. She said, "Can we go back up there for some more of those?" It was always fun to take Mom and Gerry to local tourist attractions, and she especially liked to ride the Narrow Gauge railway from Cripple Creek to Victor and shop in the gift stores.

Driving past the South Platte River now and getting closer to Dead Man's Gulch, we were enjoying the scenery. The wall of mountain peaks were snow covered at the very tops. There were few clouds hanging over the peaks, all of which looked like cotton candy and barely moved. We were getting close to the fork in the lost road when I remembered Flo's Diner. Dad and I had stopped there before, so I asked Uncle Johnny if he'd like to stop there for lunch. "We packed lots of sandwiches, but I think you'd really like Flo," I said.

"If we have time to stop there, that sounds like fun." I pulled into the parking lot of the old-style diner fashioned out of a railroad dining car. There wasn't enough room in there for Sarah, so I asked her to wait out front on a small patch of grass and gave her some water. Uncle Johnny couldn't get over the way Sarah seemed to understand everything I said to her. Flo was at the cash register when we walked in and said, "Well hello, stranger! Where the hell have you been, Charlie?"

"Hi Flo, I wanted you to meet my Uncle Johnny." I smiled.

"Hi there, Uncle Johnny." She dipped her hips in a flirting way.

"Well, hi there Flo." he imitated her hip dip and we all let out a roar of laughter at the same time. I had met Flo many years before on a sales trip. I had worked as a sales rep for a manufacturing company and made a sales trip once a month to Buena Vista, Salida, Canon City, and Jefferson. Flo's place was a normal stop for lunch and we had become good friends. We were always telling jokes to each other and I liked to tell her funny stories about my customers. Flo brought us over to a nice table overlooking the parking lot where Sarah was already napping.

"Business looks kind of slow today, Flo. Can you join us for lunch?" I asked.

"Sure I can, Charlie. I have a nice steak bone in the kitchen. I'll bring it out to Sarah first." Sarah looked up immediately when she saw Flo coming out the front door with that bone. She jumped up and down like she was saying, *Oh boy, oh boy!* Flo loved Sarah and Sarah loved her right back every bit as much.

Uncle Johnny and I sat there chuckling at the sight of them next to each other. Sarah was as big as Flo. Flo was a petite and attractive woman of Hispanic origin. She always wore the 1950s-style waitress outfit in a classy way. Her big brown eyes were captivating and her smile was as contagious as her everlasting good attitude.

As Flo returned to our table, she asked, "You going back up to that gulch, Charlie?"

"Yah, how did you know?" I responded.

"Well Charlie, you aren't exactly dressed for a wedding. It's Saturday, so I know you aren't pretending to be a salesman today."

Laughing, I said to Uncle Johnny, "I never thought of myself as a pretty boy salesman type, so I've always told Flo I was pretending."

Uncle Johnny replied, seeing his chance, "You got that right, Charlie. You're sure not a pretty boy." He tried to hold back a laugh.

"Yah Johnny, but he sure is ruggedly handsome," Flo inserted. Now we were all laughing.   "What are you guys in the mood for?" Flo asked. "I made some of my hot green chili this morning, Charlie."

"Ooh, that sounds real good to me."

Uncle Johnny asked, "What's it made from? I've never tried green chili."

Flo answered, "Well honey, you have just got to try it. It has pork, tomatoes, onions, green chiles and my special seasonings. It will surely keep the chill out of your bones for the rest of the day, at least."

"Okay, I love danger. I'll give it a try," Uncle Johnny replied. "You must if you're going up to that gulch with Charlie. Have you seen that big grizzly up there lately, Charlie?" Flo winked toward me.

"Not lately Flo, but I'm ready for him if I do." I flashed my Swiss Army knife. Now our table was roaring with laughter and so was the couple at the table next to us.

As we ate lunch, I could see the sweat dripping off of Uncle Johnny's forehead. "Damn, this is good, Flo," he said.

"You won't think so tomorrow morning." She was tickled with her timing.

"Uh oh, that does sound dangerous." He had a *you got me* expression on his face.

As we said goodbye to Flo, I asked her if she had heard the weather report for the weekend. "Yes Charlie, you had better get out of that gulch before dark. The weatherman said there is a front coming over the mountains from Utah. He also said there was a possibility of snow showers, but you know what can happen when they say that."

"No worries Flo, we'll make sure of that," I assured her.

"It was especially nice to meet you, Flo. I'm sure I'll remember you tomorrow," Uncle Johnny said.

"Nice to meet you too, Johnny. Watch out for that bear." Flo chuckled.

Before we drove away, Uncle Johnny said, "I sure could use one of those cold beers in the cooler."

"Sure! You deserve one after getting down all of that hot green chili." I got a cold one for him and drove toward the gulch—and hopefully the answers to all my treasure questions. As we arrived at the entrance to the canyon where the gulch was, I noticed the trees had lost many leaves and I could see more of the canyon. I hadn't been there this late in the year before. There was a lot of wildlife activity. The birds and squirrels were out for their daily gathering. I had to stop to get Uncle Johnny another cold one and one for me too. "That green chili made me thirsty too," I quipped.

"You aren't kidding!" he said. While I opened the back of the Jeep, I heard Uncle Johnny say, "Look at that! Did you see that, Charlie?"

"What?"

"Up on that rocky hilltop, a bear crossed between the rocks."

"What color was it?"

"Brown, I think. Could it be a grizzly?" he asked with urgency and more than a little worry.

"Could be, but Flo was just teasing. There aren't too many grizzlies around Colorado these days. For the most part, they have been seen in Wyoming."

"What did they do, build a big fence up on the border so they couldn't come down here? If it's just the same to you, you had better keep that Swiss Army knife handy. I'm not scared of him."

"Me either," I said as we both laughed at each other.

It was a bumpy ride with all the ruts made by the rainstorms. I could see plentiful animal foot prints in the hardened mud. Many of the prints were deer tracks. I wasn't sure about what had made some of the other tracks. It must have been very large though, I thought.

Uncle Johnny noticed the tracks, too. "Charlie, if you don't have grizzlies up here, you must have a bigfoot!"

"The water level in the river is low. That's good news for us. We have a better chance to find some gold. I'm going to look for that place where Christiana described seeing the kissing prairie dogs."

"What do you think it is?" Uncle Johnny asked.

"Well, I'm not sure, but it must be rocks, trees, a hillside, or some land mark with good visibility."

"Yah well, we had better keep our eyes open for everything up here." He had a serious tone of voice.

"Yes indeed. This hasn't exactly been the safest place for me." I parked in my usual spot and quickly went to the back of the Jeep to let Sarah out.

"What are we going to do first?" Uncle Johnny asked.

"Why don't we look for a spot to pan for nuggets, then after awhile I want to look for those prairie dogs," I said.

"That sounds like a great plan to me."

"Let's get the gear out of the Jeep and head upstream. I remember a place a short distance up the path where there is a bend in the river. It should be a good place to start." I knew it was a likely place for gold to settle. The water level was low enough that it gave me reason for optimism. I felt lucky and all the conditions were right. I found the spot and right away saw some black sand behind a big boulder. The monster rock had been sitting in the river, but was now to the side because of the low water level.

"Here we are, Uncle Johnny. I'll get the shovel out. Here is the gold pan. Let's see how good your training was. This is exactly the kind of place in a river where gold is found." I explained how gold flows down the river. We found gold dust in less than twenty minutes. Uncle Johnny was excited and I gave him one of the bottles to put it in. Relieved that Uncle Johnny would have some gold to take home, I started thinking about looking for the real treasure. "Way to go, Uncle Johnny. If you don't mind I'll take a walk with Sarah and see what I can find while you're getting rich down here."

"Hell no! That's fine. I'll watch the cold beer for us. Did you take your knife, Charlie?"

"Yah, and save one of those cold ones for me when I get back. Come on, Sarah." We went up the side of the eastern foothill. Just before we got out of sight I heard Uncle Johnny call out.

"I got a nugget here, Charlie. Come back and look at this!" He was whooping it up.

"Okay, be right there." When I got back over to him, even I was surprised.

He handed it to me and I said with astonishment, "I'll be damned, you sure as hell do. Congratulations, Uncle Johnny. That's a beauty." Looking over the nugget, I realized he'd found a nice-looking nugget—close to two troy ounces, I guessed.

"How much do you think it is worth, Charlie?"

"Well, gold is over four hundred dollars an ounce now. This seems about two ounces and nuggets are worth more than gold dust. I think you might get over a thousand dollars for it," I responded.

"Wow, this is fun."

"Where exactly did you find it?" I asked.

"I found it behind that big boulder, where the water level stops."

"You might want to dig down to the bed rock and see if you can find some more," I recommended.

"Damn right I will, Charlie." Uncle Johnny smiled the biggest grin I had ever seen. That was about the time I noticed a big dark cloud coming over us. The birds and squirrels had disappeared. Uncle Johnny looked up at the cloud, too. "Do we need to be worried about the snow flurries in the air?"

"Yah, they sure are snow flurries, but I think we have time for you to find another nugget and for me to have a quick look for those prairie dogs. Okay, I'll head back up that hill." Sarah let out a bark. She stayed close to me as we got out of Uncle Johnny's sight.

The hill was a lot steeper than it looked from down below, and the going was slow. Sarah stayed close behind as the walking darn near turned into climbing. Some of the snow stuck to the ground as the temperature dipped. It was making me nervous, but I had to see what was on that next slope. Something kept pushing me higher and higher. Then the magic moment came. I spotted a grove of scrub oak stripped of its leaves. Under the bare trees I could finally see the kissing prairie dogs. It was a rock formation with the tops of two boulders connecting. It really did have the shape of two prairie dogs kissing. I was very excited, and my adrenaline started pumping. "There it is, girl," I told Sarah. The distance was a couple of hundred yards further up the mountain. The snow was an inch deep now, but I was determined to get up there. We had a Jeep and could drive out with a four-wheel drive. Up we went.

I stopped to rest on a rock for a minute and catch my breath. Then I realized the nugget Uncle Johnny had found might have been from the treasure. I wondered if the heavy rains had washed the nuggets out of their hiding place or if that nugget was from another source. I shouldn't have been thinking about other things at that time, though. As I got up to get started again, my left foot lost its footing and I started to tumble out of control down the steep side of the mountain, crashing over everything below me. I landed hard on my left foot and felt immediate and terrible pain. It felt like it might have been broken and certainly hurt very bad. Sarah was barking nonstop at the top of her voice as she came down to me. I was in a fix now, still halfway up the hillside. I was in pain and unable to walk. All I could do was hope Uncle Johnny could hear Sarah's loud barking. It wasn't very long before I could hear Uncle Johnny call out, "Where are you, Charlie? Are you up there?"

"I'm up here!" I yelled back as Sarah barked.

Uncle Johnny made it up the mountain where I was and asked while catching his breath, "What the hell happened?"

"I guess I took a bad step."

"I guess so." He frowned.

Trying to keep my sense of humor, I said with a painful gasp, "That was athletic, don't you think?"

"I didn't see it, but if you say so."

I pointed to where I was and told him I had spotted the prairie dogs.

"You sure as hell aren't getting up there today, Charlie. It's going to be tough getting you out of here. Can you walk?"

"I can't put any weight on it at all. It hurts too much," I said with dismay.

"I'll have to find a crutch for you because I don't think I can carry you down that steep hill."

"Okay, that sounds like a good plan," I said in ever-worsening pain.

Just as Uncle Johnny turned to go on his search he said, "Ah crap! Don't look now, but that really is a grizzly. He's up there where you just fell from."

As I looked up I realized the fall might have saved me and Sarah from a deadly encounter with that bear. It must have heard the barking and came for a look. Sarah smelled the bear and started barking wildly. Uncle Johnny waved his hands in the air and yelled at the bear. He grabbed my Swiss Army knife and yelled up at the bear, "You'd better not come down here! I got a Swiss Army knife. Do you see this? I'll cut you up into little pieces!" he was pretty damn serious. If it wasn't such a scary moment, I would have started laughing. The bear looked down on us with wide-open jaws and let out a terrific roar of his own. I knew Sarah couldn't beat a bear that big and ferocious. I worried about her.

"Stay where you are, Sarah." The moment of decision came for the bear and he went on his way. Uncle Johnny had just run the best bluff I'd ever seen. If he wasn't bluffing, he was the tough guy I needed to have around that day.

Uncle Johnny sat down in the snow next to me for a minute. "You are some tour guide, Charlie. Do you have this much fun every time you go hunting for gold?"

"Yah, look at all of the fun you've been missing out on." I tried to get out a laugh in the midst of my pain.

"Let's get you the hell away from all of this fun for now." Uncle Johnny walked away and came back with a stick suitable to help me hobble down the hill. As slow going as it was, I was just glad to be going.

"Did you find any more nuggets?" I asked.

"I found this little one." He pulled a nugget out of his pocket twice the size of the first one, smiling with a wide grin.

"It was worth your trouble, I hope," I said to him.

"What trouble do you mean? This was a lot of fun."

By the time we got to the Jeep, we were both tired and I was in a lot of pain. Uncle Johnny helped me into the passenger seat. "I don't think you're in any shape to drive, so I guess I will."

"Okay, then, I'll take that cold beer now if you can get me one." I enjoyed every sip of it. The snow was getting pretty deep. Uncle Johnny put the Jeep in four-wheel drive and we got out of there. I asked Uncle Johnny to stop back by Flo's diner to see if she had any strong pain pills for my ankle.

"I don't think it's broken. Maybe it's just a bad sprain."

"I hope that is all that it is. I know there are not any hospitals up here." After what seemed like a long drive we arrived at the diner. It was after dark now and Flo was closing the diner when we got there.

"Charlie, did you get into a fight with that grizzly bear?" she quizzed me.

"Damn near," I said with a sigh.

"He's not kidding, Flo," Uncle Johnny added.

"Well then, let's get you inside and fix you up a little." She helped me in.

"That idea sounds great to me, Flo. Do you have any powerful aspirin?"

"I have something better than that." She dug out two 800-milligram ibuprofen pills from her purse.

"You are awesome, Flo." I was grateful.

"Don't I know it, Charlie. Don't I just know." She laughed all the way back to the kitchen. When she returned, she had a bottle of my favorite whiskey in her hand. "I've been saving this for a special occasion. I guess with all of that snow out there and you in that condition, this is as special an occasion as it gets." She opened the bottle and made three drinks. "You know, I have the basement prepared for an occasion such as this. There are beds down there with a shower and a television. It's warm and comfortable. Why don't you guys stay here the night in this dangerous weather?"

I quickly responded, "I think I've had enough danger for the day. How about you, have you had enough fun yet today, Uncle Johnny?"

"Are you kidding? I'm good to go on that danger thing for a while." He shrugged. There was good chemistry between the three of us. There was always a laugh about to happen.

"Great! I'll get the phone so you can call Meredith. I hope she won't be too upset," Flo said.

"I think she'll be fine with it. She's easygoing and likes to stay informed. She's adapted well to my adventures by now."

"I don't know how anyone can get used to your adventures, Charlie," Flo sighed.

Dialing the phone, I tried to clear the pain from my voice so I wouldn't worry Meredith. She answered, "Is that you, Charlie?"

"Oh, hi honey! How's it going?" I asked.

"I'm fine," Meredith answered as if she was waiting for the other shoe to drop. "Where are you?"

"We're at Flo's diner. We got delayed a little."

"The weatherman said it's snowing up there. You had better stay up there and not chance it."

"That's a good idea. We were thinking the same thing," I agreed.

"How did your search go?"

"Uncle Johnny found two nice gold nuggets and I was able to see the kissing prairie dogs, although I didn't get a chance to get up to it. There was just a little problem with a fall down the hill side and a grizzly bear." I added nonchalantly.

"Are you alright?" She was worried.

"Oh yah, just a little sprained ankle, that's all," minimizing the fright factor as much as possible. Meredith knew better.

"How bad is it?"

"I can't walk on it, but it's not broken."

"When are you going to stop getting into those dangerous predicaments?" she said in a deep negative tone.

"You know me Meredith, I always come out okay," I joked.

"I guess so, but I don't know how you do it." To my relief, she poked fun back at me.

"Just lucky, I guess. I'll call you in the morning with our plan. How's Mariah?" I gladly changed the conversation.

"She's fine. She loves the kitty Bobo. I'll talk to you tomorrow. I love you," she reassured me.

"Bye, I love you too." I said as we hung up. Flo and Uncle Johnny looked at me with a grin.

"You made that seem like it was no big deal." Uncle Johnny smirked and we all laughed.

"Will you two give me a push down the stairs? I'd like to get that foot up in the air," I joked.

"Hey Flo! Why don't we send him down the laundry chute?" Uncle Johnny said with a big grin. "Is that alright with you, Charlie?" They both laughed and helped me down to the basement.

Getting comfortable, Flo asked me, "Charlie, there are some books over here on this shelf. Would you like to read one?"

"Sure, what do you have?" She read off some titles. One in particular got my interest. Flo said,   "This one is *Life with the Gold Miners* by Chief Joseph Tall Horse.

"I'll try that one."

Flo and Uncle Johnny went upstairs to finish their drinks and put something on the stove for dinner. As I started reading, optimism permeated my being and laughter entered my thoughts. It surely was a difficult environment for those Cripple Creek and Leadville miners, working hundreds of feet below the ground. Yet they still found ways to enjoy life and get along well with the American Indians among them.

The first event Chief Joseph Tall Horse spoke of was the craziest thing I had ever heard of—if you can imagine forty gold miners standing above a hole in the ground on a Sunday afternoon with sticks of dynamite in their hands. The idea was to hold the lighted sticks of dynamite longer than your challenger before throwing it into the hole. Chief Joseph Tall Horse tells of big wagers during these games and a few men who lost fingers betting on their own courage, which at times was excessive. The chief said, "Those crazy miners were braver than General George Custer."

He said he would get drunk often and listen to the stories of some of the miners. "I get drunk much and hear tall stories." Sometimes they would tell him how they got pieces of gold out of the mine without anyone knowing. Then, when they sobered up, they would have to buy him more whiskey to keep his silence. The chief said there was an annual fair near Cripple Creek and Victor that cost ten cents for entry. They would have lots of games and events. As many as ten thousand people lived in the region at the time. The chief said that he had much fun with the white men. "On fair days, I wait for them to get drunk and find many dimes on the ground."

The whiskey and pain pills must have gotten to me about then, because I went to sleep and didn't wake up until the next morning. The snow stopped falling and the sun was shining bright, as is often the case in Colorado. Weather events come and go quickly. My ankle was hurting, but I was in good spirits. I found the kissing prairie dogs and was one step closer to the hidden treasure, I hoped. Uncle Johnny had a great memory and two gold nuggets. Flo had some laughs and a memory of her own. As we said goodbye that morning, I had the feeling she and Uncle Johnny had formed an everlasting bond. We drove home to Meredith and Mariah and enjoyed a relaxing day on the couch.

My ankle healed over the next week. The injury prevented me from working as an outside salesman, so I drove Uncle Johnny around to some of the tourist attractions, which he thoroughly enjoyed. I took him to a nearby ghost town, which gave us both a chill with its abandoned buildings and streets. I also, had a chance to take him to see my friends at the coin store where he received a check for $3,200. He was one happy camper. He offered to share it with me, but I insisted that he deserved it and I was after a much bigger treasure. When I took Uncle Johnny to the airport, we laughed all the way about the grizzly bear and how he scared it away with my Swiss Army knife. "Were you really serious?" I asked.

"Hell yeah, that bear didn't want to mess around with me! He would have been one hurting puppy." He was still laughing as he walked down the aisle to his plane.

CHAPTER FOURTEEN

I was feeling the lonely emptiness I always feel whenever someone in my family visits and returns back to their home, but my spirits were high and I was ready to spend some more time in the library and museum. I knew the mounting snow in Dead Man's Gulch would prevent me from going back up there until April or May at the earliest. I could hardly wait to get up to the place Christiana had called kissing prairie dogs and had promised I could see the hidden treasure from. I dreamed about it often that winter, but satisfied myself with good finds from my research. My first find for that winter came in November, just before Thanksgiving. I had extra time off, so I used the opportunity to spend a day at the local Penrose Library.

I didn't feel like working hard that day, so I went into the local history section and started browsing. I found a book written by Sassy Langdon in 1912. It was titled *My Life with Trapper Joe in Park County*. It seemed intriguing and I wanted to learn more about that region. As I started reading, I was glad to see the book started out forty-seven years before the time of her writing it in 1865. That was the time I wanted to know more about.

It began, *It was a great life Joe Langdon and I had back then in the early days. It was the spring of 1865 when I met Joe in a saloon down Pueblo way. He had just come in from a trip up to the mountains from a place called Beaver Creek. He sure had a pack horse loaded down with those pristine beaver pelts and was raring for a whoop-it-up party. My profession as a dance hall entertainer bore out the fact that I loved a good party at every opportunity. I hadn't met Joe before, but took particular notice to the fact that he cleaned up real well for a mountain man. Joe seemed to take hold of me with his eyes that night and he never did let go. We flopped in my room that lovely evening, which was a whirlwind romance for even me. Those blue eyes of his could tell me any story I wanted to hear and make every dream come true. That load of beaver pelts he brought back with him had fetched a pretty good sum of money down at Jack's Trading Post. He already had marriage in his plans.*

"I've got a darn good stake here, Sassy. Enough for us to get a good start in them there hills, if you be in an agreeable mind to hitch your wagon to mine."

"Now Joe, you've been up in those mountains a long time without the company of a woman. I don't know if you know your own mind so soon."

"Oh yes, darling, believe in me that I sure do know my own mind and I sure enough want to marry you this very day. Now what do you say to that?"

"Joe, I could see myself married to you, but I don't know about living alone up in those mountains. I like living with fun and excitement once in a while and some good company."

"We can fix that, darling. I'll just build you a saloon up there in the

South Park, right next to the South Platte River where all them other trappers could come by once in a while and need a place to spend their money," Joe said in a matter-of-fact manner. That was all I wanted to hear and that started my wonderful life with trapper Joe Langdon in Park County, Colorado.

That was an enjoyable book, front to back, but it had some special information for me. In the middle of the book Sassy talked about going on a trip with Joe to trade beaver belts with Suu Tavaci, Chief of the Ute Indian Tribe in a place called Dead Man's Gulch. "We went up there to a place I could never find again. When we arrived at their camp, there was much dancing and celebration going on all about. Joe was one of very few white men who were welcomed at that camp, because he had become a trusted trading partner. He was allowed to sit in council with Suu Tavaci and speak of the events of the day. I have a good memory of Chief Suu Tavaci's wife, Mamaci Paa and am quite certain that she was a white woman. I am not certain how her trail led to where she was and of that she would not say. She was very gracious and showed me how she made the moccasins that she had traded for a Beaver pelt with Joe. Before we left there she asked that I not speak of her, because she was very happy with her life and did not want to be disturbed. I agreed to her request and only today do I speak of her. That was all Sassy wrote about Suu Tavaci and Mamaci Paa, but it was fun to hear of another event in Christiana's life.

On a beautiful sunny day in December, at the Denver Public Library, I found a shocking article that brought me closer to the end of my quest for Mamaci Paa's descendants. The headline read: *News from Grand Junction tells of the death of Ute Indian chief.*

The article continued: *Chief Maiku was killed in an unusual horse riding accident recently. Spectators of a horse race recently held with the Ute Indian tribe and townspeople of this region report that the chief was leading the activities and participating in a horse race when he became a victim of an unfortunate and sudden accident. His champion horse stumbled in a creek bed and came down on him. He was believed to have suffered a broken neck in the accident. His heartbroken wife, Mary Rivet, and their daughter Philemon, are reportedly grief-stricken. The chief had no sons and it is unknown who the new chief will be. A ceremony will be held for Maiku at the Garden of the Gods where he will rest with his mother and father, Suu Tavaci and Mamaci Paa, and his grandfather, Wacuwini Muatagoci.*

I needed to get home from Denver early that evening, so I left immediately after reading this article. We were having good friends over for dinner that night which we hadn't seen for quite a while. Jim is a history teacher at one of the local high schools and Cindy is a director for the preschool program at the community college. It was good to see them again and we had great conversation over lasagna dinner. At some point, Jim left the bar where we usually have dinner with friends, and went to use the upstairs bathroom. Upon his return, he nonchalantly asked who the lady was in that room. Meredith and I were quite surprised as we had not mentioned Christiana to anyone, other than Uncle Johnny. I asked Jim to describe her for us and, without much surprise, he described Christiana just as I had to Meredith the first time.

With this revelation, we spent the next part of the night telling

Jim and Cindy the whole story about Christiana. That gave them a surprise, but both were in total agreement that Christiana was indeed real and was in our home—at least from time to time. Meredith and I were convinced now that I hadn't just been seeing a ghost, but that she really did exist. Sometimes it's nice to know you aren't crazy.

After Jim and Cindy bid us goodbye, Meredith and I went to the bathroom and looked for Christiana. She wasn't there. It would seem that she decided when people were to see her and she had a plan for the big picture. I wish she could have told me what to do next. I really didn't have a clue where to go. I only knew the names of people I needed to find out about and if they had other children. I looked everywhere I could think of for articles or obituaries of Mary and Philemon Rivet and found nothing whatsoever.

I spent most of February getting nowhere at any of the libraries, college, or museum. That's when Meredith came to my rescue in her low key, matter-of-fact way. It was a cold and snowy night. We had the fireplace going and I made chili on the stove. Mariah was warm and cozy and wrapped up on the couch. I was playing some oldies on the stereo. I was telling Meredith about my frustrations getting any further with my research and she blurted out, "Where was this Mary Rivet from? Maybe she went home after Maiku's death." What a simple idea I hadn't thought of! I was so wrapped up in the investigation that I couldn't see the forest for the trees. "That could well be what happened." I continued, "She may have gone there for security. With Maiku gone, she may not have had a high place in the tribe any longer, nor any support." Then I said, "Meredith, I have got to go to Glens Falls, New York."

She replied, "You sure do, Charlie."

CHAPTER FIFTEEN

I was on an airplane the next week. I didn't have much time off work, but I was hoping four days would be enough. I was laughing at myself for how much trouble I would go through and yet I hadn't done any research about my own family history. I had heard stories from Grandma when I was young about how she was part French and part Iroquois Indian, but I really didn't know any more than that about her parents and grandparents or my grandfather's relatives either. I thought it was a neat coincidence they were from Glens Falls and my dad was born where I was headed to research Mary and Philemon Rivet. Their names were similar in that Grandma's last name was Rivers, so I thought I'd have a look at my own ancestors while I was there.

My brother Roger and his wife Carol picked me up at the airport and brought Uncle Johnny along. Their motor home gave me a place to sleep. We would also be comfortable for all of the driving we were going to do. I flew into Connecticut to visit there before we went to New York. Uncle Johnny was happy because we would pass close by Uncle Joe's where he often traveled for great chili dogs. I wanted a few of those too and I knew we would all have plenty of laughs. I wasn't in the motor home five minutes when Roger asked me if I had remembered my Swiss Army knife, just in case Uncle Johnny needed it. He said, "Charlie, I don't know about you. Ever since you were a little boy you were always getting into one jam or another. I don't know how many times I've rescued you myself. I wish you'd be a little less adventurous."

Carol followed up with, "Yah, but Roger, he always seems to get out of trouble somehow."

Uncle Johnny said, "Well, I don't know what he would have done if I didn't tell that grizzly a thing or two." They were all laughing and I laughed right along with them.

By the time we reached Carol and Roger's house in a little town called Chaplin, everyone knew the whole story about Christiana and Dead Man's Gulch. I don't think Roger believed in the ghost, but he humored me nonetheless. I had almost forgotten how thick the forests were there. Even in late winter, visibility was only hundreds of yards instead of miles like in Colorado. I didn't remember the air being so heavy. It was nice to go by places I had been to in my past, though. The old dairy farms hadn't changed a bit. The streets were littered with Italian restaurants and I had sure missed the great food. The clouds hung low and thick, and the sun was a slight image of itself as I knew it living way up high in Colorado. Roger and Carol's house was always a treat to visit. He always loved animals and had many of them, including horses, rabbits, chickens, goats, pheasants, and even some pigs from time to time. It was truly Roger's farm in the country. Oh yah, he even had peacocks, too.

When we walked into the house, I was happy to see some of

my many cousins there to greet me. We had a mini family reunion. There was Debbie, Rene, Ronnie, and Robbie, along with my old fishing buddy Rebecca. little Ray, Alan, Cindy, Wayne, Marcy, Fran, Charlotte and Denyce were also there with Aunt Mary and all of their wives, husbands, and kids. There were also my other brothers and sisters, Shelly, Kathy, Gary, Scott and their wives, husbands, and kids. Finally, Mom and Gerry were also in attendance. We would have needed a big recreation hall for the many more that weren't there. They had prepared a feast for a king and had lots of cold beer. Every one should have a family like ours; our grandparents George and Pearl made with no small sacrifice. There were many stories from long ago and it was standing room only.

I wondered how near-tragic events could become so funny years later. Like the story Mary told about Grandma Pearl and her bear on the front porch of the old school house. I was there the next day and can verify what Grandma said about the bear. In this case it was a black bear. I'm sure there aren't any grizzlies in Connecticut; well, maybe not completely sure.

Grandma said, "That son of a bitch got up on that front porch thinking he was going to come in and get something to eat. I had news for him. I got my broom out and swatted him a couple times before he got the idea. Ha, ha! I showed him." Grandma's vocabulary expanded to swear words in times of fun and excitement.

There were many more stories about Grandma Pearl and Grandpa George. Grandpa had so many kids to support that he would go off to the city of Hartford on weekends and get into exhibition boxing matches to make extra money. I guess he was a tough fighter because his record was 44-0. It was said he sparred with the great Willie Pep. The stories about grandma catching chickens in the backyard for dinner, cutting their heads off, and de-feathering them were true. I'd seen her do it. It's also true that grandma snuffed tobacco, smoked filter-less cigarettes, and drank as many quarts of beer that she could get. She also cussed up a storm with the greatest sense of humor you could ever hear. She lived through one of her babies dying from an oxygen tent fire in the hospital and two of her houses lost to fire, including the old school house. One of her sons, my dad, spent two years in a hospital suffering from polio, among many other serious crises. When she died, over 300 people existed because of her. How's that for a life?

The next day we headed for Glens Falls in Roger's motor home. With Uncle Johnny and his sense of humor in tow, we couldn't go wrong. Most importantly, for the sake of this trip we brought along my cousin Charlotte, who is Rebecca's sister. The day before I found out she had been working on our family history. I thought she could help me with my research while she was getting more information for our own family. Her dad, Uncle Francis, was a smart guy with electronics and other things. He was the guy in the family who would go out to our homes on a Sunday night or whenever and repair a bad tube in the earliest models of television sets so we could watch the "Honeymooners" or "Rawhide". I learned she was becoming well known for her research prowess and wrote a weekly local history article for the newspaper in the town she lived in. Charlotte and I thought the similarities between Grandma's last name of Rivers and Mary's last name of Rivet was curious, but then again they both had French ancestors. I was in a hurry to get there and see what we could find out about Mary and Philemon, but we had to stop off on South Street when we got to town for some of those one-of-a-kind chili dogs.

Glens Falls is a town of 14,000 and it had actually changed names several times since the early 1700s. It was originally called Chepontuc by the Iroquois Indians meaning "difficult place to get around," because of the rocky countryside. The town was also called Great Carrying Place, The Corners, and Wings Falls before it was named Glens Falls after Col Johannes Glen in 1788. The town was the site of many battles during the French-Indian war and the Revolutionary War. The town was located between Fort Edward and William Henry and was mostly destroyed by fire twice. The local Quakers abandoned the town until after the Revolutionary War in 1783.

When we arrived at the Crandall Public Library, the weather was overcast and we were all in good spirits. Roger, Carol, and Uncle Johnny dropped us off and then they went to go sightsee and visit relatives. This was the equivalent of sightseeing for Charlotte and me, and maybe a little more exciting for us. We caught on quick as to where the information was situated and got right to work, she on Rivers/Gauldin and me on Rivet/Tavaci. We really had fun. I could see the glow on Charlotte's face in between the book racks. We had some problems, though. Charlotte learned many of the French people went back and forth across the Canadian border without documentation. The French language was translated differently and it was, at the very least, difficult to figure out who was who. We decided to look at the obituaries and then verify birth certificates at the town hall. I was happy to see Charlotte make terrific progress, and by the end of that day she found much of our family information, up to grandma and grandpa's parents: Robert Moses Rivers married Louise Besaw and John Paul Gauldin married Rosalie Montville.

I did not fare so well and only found the birth announcement for Mary Rivet. Still, it was something. Her parents were Colonel Raymond and Elenore Bush Rivet. I found no other information for that family and felt dejected. However, I was encouraged by Charlotte's research progress and it was fun to find out about my own family.

Roger, Carol, and Uncle Johnny picked us up at the town hall, which was close by. It was closing time and we started the trip back to Connecticut. Charlotte was elated and recited to us what she found most of the way back. Carol asked, "Does this mean you get to come back again?"

"I hope so, but, I'd find an excuse to come back no matter what had happened," I assured her.

"Yah, he can come out here and get in trouble just as easy as he can there," Uncle Johnny said, laughing.

Roger followed up, "If he comes back here to get in trouble, he at least knows he has us here to get him out, just like always. Ha, ha!"

Charlotte giggled at us the whole time. "You guys are too funny."

With the lack of good ideas on what to do next, we decided to spend the next day at the ocean. My sisters, Kathy and Shelley, were happy to go along on this trip. We stopped at Charleston for some much-needed clamming. Kathy and Shelley easily bagged a full cooler by themselves. The rest of us matched their prowess and bagged another bushel or so. We were wading out in the bay and just as a crab was taste-testing my big toe, Kathy said, "Hey Charlie, bet you don't have this much fun in Colorado."

Shelley followed up, "Yah, Charlie, bet you don't have any of these in Colorado."

"Not a single one," I said. "We only have lions and bears."

"Yah, right, and you seem to find them pretty easily, Charlie," Kathy said.

The next stop was Judith Pointe where the lobster fishermen come back to the docks with their day's catch. By the time we got there it was pouring rain and the fishermen didn't want to hang around very long. I offered one hundred dollars for twenty lobsters and a fisherman accepted it on the spot. He even offered to deliver them to our car—now that's living! We had a feast for the ages that night at Roger's house and laughs by the bucketful. By the next evening, I was back home, full of memories and worrying about my mission for Christiana.

CHAPTER SIXTEEN

Undaunted by my failure, the very next day I was at the museum looking for any clue. My education about the old west, Ute Indian tribe, and the gold miners of the time was increasing, but my knowledge about Christiana's family was only gaining in tidbits. Still, I was too stubborn to give up. I read many articles that had nothing to do with my research in order to learn and get inspired with the right idea about where to take the next step. I read about some of the gold hunter's trips and disappointments back in the 1800s, some with very tragic consequences. Many settlers lost their lives chasing their dreams and many more found their dreams chasing their life's trail. As for me, I felt like I was chasing my life's tail and going in circles. By now I was lost in a void and stuck in a vacuum of indecision. I really didn't know what to do or where to go to finish my mission. March and April came and went and the snow in the mountains had begun melting. The time was coming for me to go back to Dead Man's Gulch soon. I began to look forward to it. I think Sarah was getting restless, too. She begged at the front door quite often.

It was early on a Monday morning during the first week of May when I awoke to another whisper. "Get the gold, Charlie.

Others search." I jolted wide awake. The flickering light from the television pulsed in and out. It made me wonder if Christiana had been there. I wondered if it was just my imagination. I worried that maybe someone else was indeed after the lost treasure of Dead Man's Gulch again. Why not? Many have searched for over 120 years. I didn't think they had found it, but I wasn't sure. Was someone getting close to finding the treasure? There were many people who'd heard about it. Those two snakes of men I ran into up there had heard about it in jail or somewhere.

I waited until six o'clock when Flo opened her diner on the mountain. Then I called her on the telephone. "Hi Flo, how are you?" I asked cheerfully.

"Just fine, how about you? It's great to hear from you."

"Well, I need to go back to the gulch. Has the snow melted yet?" I hoped for a yes.

"Charlie, you are crazy! Are you really going to do that? Most of the snow is gone, but I think there's still some in the gulch. Wait, Charlie . . . I have to tell you something. You'd better be careful if you go back up there. A couple of people came in for breakfast last week and they were asking a lot of questions about that gulch and where it's located. The guy that came in looked like a real gorilla, and the girl he was with was scary. She had mean eyes and acted sneaky. She whispered to him a lot. He had a scruffy beard and evil tattoos on his neck."

"Oh." I paused to think. "I wonder if he heard about it down at the prison where those other guys are?"

"That could be what happened, Charlie. I have to get the diner ready to open. Will you stop in if you come up?" she asked with hope.

"Sure Flo, I'll see you then. Bye." After that phone call, I knew it wasn't just my imagination worrying me. I knew the whisper I heard was real.

I thought better of going up there again right away, though. I had enough danger for a while and sure didn't want to tangle with an avalanche. I stopped worrying about those other treasure hunters finding the treasure. They couldn't do it either with snow on the ground and I didn't think anyone had found it in 120 years even without snow on the ground. I decided to wait a couple of more weeks and then I'd call Ranger Garrison to ask about the snow. In the meantime I took a break from thinking about any of it. That was the best thing I could do. I spent some time with Meredith and Mariah and cleared my busy head. Two weeks later, I called the ranger and asked about the snow. He told me it should be gone in another week and he'd keep on eye up there for any more bad guys. That was comforting.

The following Saturday I took Meredith and Mariah over to Old Colorado City for lunch. There is a Mexican restaurant there which makes the best chili rellenos I had ever tasted. On the way out, we turned to walk down the street to a chocolate shop and what I saw enlightened and reinvigorated me. Just out front of a trading post gift shop was a wooden statue of an army cavalry officer and one of a Ute Indian in full head dress. It was at that moment that everything clicked for me. I knew where Mary Rivet went with Philemon, or at least what she went to. Seeing those statues made me remember she had been an interpreter for the government with Indian tribes. She may very well have gone back to doing what she knew best for a living and I'll bet the government would have been glad to have her. Now I had a place to look and was back in the library the very next day.

I looked in books about peace treaties. There were many of them and the only way to research the right way was to start reading all of the books about treaties and negotiations and Indian Reservations. There may have been even just a footnote with her name that I didn't want to miss. I started with events in Colorado, Utah, Wyoming, New Mexico, and Kansas. I was hoping if she did return to her old profession, it was in this region. She did know the Utes well, but the language was similar to other tribes in the west. I soon learned there were so many events with so many Indian tribes that this would be a long process for me. I decided to have fun and pick a book, any book. I skimmed the books for information about interpreters and government commissioners. I found many in the 1800s along with details on clashes and peace treaties.

When I started reading a book about the Treaty of Medicine Lodge in 1867, I found a clue, not about where Mary Rivet went to, but where she had come from. This gathering of over ten thousand people near a small lodge in eastern Kansas took place with commissioners and thirteen different Indian tribes to determine boundaries for the tribes at the Red River. The 7th Calvary was there to protect the whites and thousands of Indians were there as well. Reporters and photographers came from all over the east to report on the events. There were also many interpreters present and involved with the tribe negotiations. Many of these tribes did not want to live as the white men did, in houses and as farmers. Chief White Bear of the Kiowa was adamantly against abandoning the life of his fathers and spoke with determination against any restrictions on their nomadic way of life. The tribes were allowed to vote by standing next to a civilian or a military man. After the vote, the chief lost his bid against reservations. He and many others eventually left the reservation set aside in Oklahoma and raided white settlements. It was during the several days of these meetings that many more events were reported by the newspaper men.

I got a lucky break thanks to one of those newspaper men. It was written, *New life has been born among the talks of war and peace. On this site where so many people come together from so many nations, we have witnessed the birth of a newborn baby. In a doctor's camp tent of the 7th Cavalry, a baby was born to Colonel Raymond Rivet and his wife, who has come to be an interpreter despite her being in a family way, Elenore Bush Rivet from Glens Falls, New York. The baby will be named Mary. We are reminded by this event that despite the petty problems of men, the big story of life goes on. The birth was assisted by Doctor John Moeri and his wife, Bertha. In attendance for this event for reporting was my wife Mabel.* This news was reported by Charles Bigler of the *The Goodland Kansas News*.

I now knew how Mary had become an interpreter for the Indian Commission. It was as a result of learning from her mom's life's work. I had more clues now to look for where Mary went. I could now look for her mother and father's story researching the 7th cavalry. I had renewed optimism. If I could find an obituary for Colonel Raymond Rivet or his wife, Elenore, then I might find the names and locations of their family. I went right to the section in the library where I could find the history of the 7th Cavalry Regiment. I found plenty of information about them. This division was famous and infamous for many events in the 1800s, not the least of which is The Battle of Little Bighorn in 1876. The regiment had originally formed after the Civil War in 1866 at Fort Riley, Kansas. It had received its nickname of Garry Owens after the band it formed chose an Irish drinking song as its marching tune. The regiment fought in the Indian wars, the first of which was The Battle of Washita in 1868. They moved to Fort Abraham Lincoln, Nebraska in 1873 where, during the Black Hills gold rush, Colonel Custer and his men were outnumbered and killed. In 1877, during The Battle of Bear Paw, the 7th Cavalry captured Chief Joseph Nez Perce. In 1890 they perpetrated the massacre of Wounded Knee. I discovered more records were kept about the military men in the regiment.

That is exactly where I found a general order issued in 1880 by General Drum called "Promotions, Appointments, Transfers, and Casualties." Among the transfers was that of Colonel Raymond Rivet. He retired from active military service and resided in Glens Falls, New York, with his wife Elenore and their thirteen-year-old daughter, whose name was Mary. Then, in another order issued three years later by General Drum, Colonel

Raymond Rivet was reactivated, promoted to a general officer, and assigned to Fort Lewis, Colorado. The Fort was established among the Ute Indian tribes and I was now sure that this must be where Mary learned how to speak in the Ute language and also how she must have met Maiku. I was elated to know the Fort Lewis records might give me the missing pieces in my puzzle.

Maiku would have been in his late 20s and Mary would have been 16; that was old enough for a girl to marry then. I thought I might find Philemon's birth record. The article about the marriage of Maiku and Mary indicated she was from Glens Falls, but she had already been an interpreter. This could only mean she had already been talking with the Iroquois Indians who inhabited that area, perhaps with her mother Elenore. I must have missed some piece of information with her mother and father back in Glens Falls about what they were doing for those three years. I thought it might be a good excuse for another trip there someday, but right now I was hot on the trail of the descendants of Christiana Mamaci Paa Fitsimmonds.

I knew now that it was likely for me to find out much more about the history of Fort Lewis and maybe a trace of Mary and Philemon. The following Saturday was my day to finally get back to Dead Man's Gulch and nothing would stop me from my trip. I was content to begin planning for that, having great confidence that I could now get all of the rest of the information about Christiana's family.

CHAPTER SEVENTEEN

Saturday came all too slowly, but as always, it did arrive. I think Sarah knew it as well. She was waiting for me at the door when I came down the stairs that morning. So was Teddy, who Meredith had called the night before and asked to go with me. She said, "Teddy, I want you to go with Charlie just in case he needs someone else to save him."

I said to her, "Oh Meredith, it isn't likely I'll have any more problems after all I've been through already. What are the odds of that?"

She said with a smile, "With you, Charlie, it's a certainty."

"Okay., I guess you're probably right as usual." I was thinking I had an ace in the hole. Teddy had a secret weapon, and it was the hook he used for an arm.

His first words to me when I came down the stairs were, "Don't worry Charlie, I brought my hook. Any trouble from anyone and I'll hook them." He showed off his hook with a smile.

"Okay, Captain Hook, let's go then." I smiled and chuckled.

We made our usual rest stops for Sarah and were at Flo's diner just in time for mid-morning brunch. Flo hadn't met Teddy before and greeted us with, "Hi Charlie! Well hello, Sarah! Who's your handsome friend, Charlie?" She shouldn't have said that. Teddy is still enamored with her until this day.

"This is Teddy. He's my secret weapon," I said with sarcasm.

Teddy responded, "That's right Flo, he needs one. It's nice to meet you."

"Nice to meet you too, Teddy. You're darn right. He needs a whole army." She laughed. "Let me get Sarah a rib bone and get her out in the shade." She walked into the kitchen.

"Come on Ted, let's get a good seat. I'm starved." I waved at him to come to a table.

"Me too, I could eat a whole buffalo," Teddy said.

"You mean you could eat a horse, Teddy." I corrected him.

"No, I'm hungrier than that." He laughed so hard that everyone in the diner heard him. Flo came over to our table.

"Well Teddy, I have some big buffalo burgers and a helping of fries. How does that sound to you?" she offered.

"Perfect! I might need lots of energy today." He graciously accepted her offer.

"Great! What are you going to have, Charlie? Do you want more of my hot green chili?" she whispered.

"Darn right! I've been looking forward to it, along with a couple of your homemade tortillas."

Flo sat down with us for a while. "How is your Uncle Johnny?" she quizzed me.

"He's fine and in good humor," I responded.

"Well Charlie, you tell him to come back and visit me. I have special plans for him," she hinted.

"Oh really, Flo? What plans?"

She smirked. "Now don't you worry about them, Charlie. You just get him back here, would you?"

"You can count on it, Flo." I said confidently.

By now Teddy realized Flo was taken and seemed a bit dejected, but he was still himself and joked and flirted with Flo a lot.

Flo kept him on his toes, asking such things as, "How was your lunch, big boy?"

Teddy replied, "Delicious! I'd like to have someone like you cooking for me all the time. Oh gee!"

As I handed Flo a twenty-dollar-bill for lunch, she said, "I haven't seen those people back in here since I talked to you on the phone, but you two will be careful, won't you?"

"Oh sure, Flo. We both have Sarah to keep us safe," I yelled on the way out to the Jeep.

As we pulled off the main road and began the trip up the dirt road into the gulch, Teddy got excited. "Do you think we'll find the gold today, Charlie?"

"Looks like most of the snow melted, except for some here and there. We have a chance to find it today, but I'll be happy to get a little closer to that hiding place, Teddy." Sarah barked as we drew close to the river side. With her head out of the back window, she sniffed the air like it was going out of style. The squirrels were out doing their chores. The leaves bloomed on the trees and an eagle soared high. The birds were more plentiful than I had ever seen, and a family of rabbits had set up a new home in the field on the entrance to the canyon. The water level flowed fast in the river again and was high on the banks. There wasn't a cloud in the sky and the smell of spring was in the air.

As I parked, I looked up at the spot on the mountain where the kissing prairie dogs were and saw snow there, but I thought I could still make it up there. "That's the first place I have to go, Teddy. Do you see up to the top of that peak? There are two rock formations coming together in the shape of two prairie dogs kissing?" I asked him.

"Hell yah I see it. That's what you meant by kissing prairie dogs," he said with wide eyes.

"That's it Ted, but I don't think you can make it up there with that arm," I cautioned.

"Sure I can make it," he said at first, then changed his mind after he thought it over. "Well, maybe not. I guess I'll just wait down here for you, Charlie."

"Good, it'll be better if you stay down here and beep the horn if you see anything suspicious."

"Oh sure, great idea," he said, reassuring he'd do a good job for me. I let Sarah out and she instinctively headed in the direction of the hill. Sarah wanted to go up that hill first to lead the way and I was happy for her to do it. I was determined not to fall this time and held my grip tight to every rock and tree limb I could get hold of. There was still some snow in places, but it was manageable. Sarah's footprints helped me know how deep it was and gave me a good place to step. Her claws left a big print in the snow. The moss had not yet started to grow on the rocks and that lessened the slipperiness. What a relief it was to not have any cactus poking into my shoes! I took a break halfway up and found a semi-comfortable rock to sit on. Sarah lay down next to me. She was happy to have a break as well. I could see Teddy waving up at us. "The coast is clear!" he yelled up at us. I waved back with a smile. Looking around, I could see the waterfall and the pond. I was wishing it was 120 years ago and I could see Christiana going in behind the waterfall to write in her diary.

After an acceptable rest, Sarah and I resumed our climb. I was gasping for more air. The altitude kept the oxygen content of the air in a depleted condition. I had to rest more often. I could barely see Teddy when we made it to kissing prairie dogs. What satisfaction it was to finally arrive! I sat down in between the beautiful prairie dogs and caught my breath. I could see another mountain range to the west and as far as you could hope to see to the east. Looking down now and concentrating on what I was seeing below, I searched for a circle. I was wondering what Christiana had meant by a circle of life and death and a first moon. All I could see was the river with the waterfalls and pond with lots of rocks with scrub oak trees scattered about. I sat there for more than two hours and could not discern anything from the clue Christiana had given me. That was disappointing. I had to wonder if something had changed in the past 120 years and if the clues were now gone, washed away, blown away. I just didn't know. I had gone through a lot of trouble to get up to that place and it all seemed for naught. I took some pictures to study later and started back down. The time was well past three o'clock by the time Sarah and I got back down to the bottom of the mountain. Teddy had my fishing pole out of the Jeep and had already caught three trout. They looked fit for a king to eat.

He was proud, saying, "How do you think Meredith will like to have trout cooked for dinner?" He grinned a big, wide grin.

"Wow, great job Teddy. We'll at least have something to take home with us." I was content.

"Yah, I hooked them," he said with a proud laugh.

"You sure did, Ted. Why don't you pack up now and we'll get home before dark."

"Sure boss," he replied in a happy tone.

As I went down the bank to grab the fish from him, he asked, "Hey wait, what's that?" He reached down where the fish had been on a stringer and pulled up a big, beautiful gold nugget like I'd never seen before. It was twice the size of Uncle Johnny's biggest gold nugget.

"Well, I'll be damned," I said with surprise.

"Is this what I think it is?" he asked in astonishment.

"You better believe it is, Teddy. You found a valuable gold nugget." I was astonished myself. "That must be worth five thousand dollars, Teddy."

"Holy cow, Holy cow!" was all he could say. I was happy for him and he was paid well for his guard duty. He kept pulling that thing out of his pocket all of the way home. When we got home he showed it to Meredith and was prouder of it than the trout. I was happy that my adventures produced dividends for people I really cared about. I kept wondering if these nuggets had once been part of the treasure or did another gold vein become exposed and trickle down the stream. Either way, Christiana's secret was paying valuable dividends.

CHAPTER EIGHTEEN

It was a happy week at my house following the trip, but I wasn't satisfied. I still had the whole summer to find Christiana's treasure and however long it took to find her family. I had to make a new plan. I relaxed and spent time with Meredith and Mariah, who was getting bigger and cuter with every day. Meredith was happy and my sales job was going very well. Colorado Springs has so much to offer in the summer. We went to the Cheyenne Mountain Zoo, Seven Falls, Cave of the Winds, and a ghost town in Old Colorado City. By now, Meredith's mom and dad, Myron and Louise, had insisted on taking Mariah for one day a week. She was already learning much from them. She started using her left hand to eat and was trying to set the table like Grandma had shown before her first birthday, moving a napkin from one place to another.

I was restless, though, and asked Meredith if she minded if Sarah and I went on another trip to Dead Man's Gulch. She insisted I take Teddy back with me since he had been good luck the first time that I went. Teddy didn't mind at all since he had a good time, caught some trout, and got a check for over five thousand dollars for his gold nugget. I didn't mind because it was nice to have a security guard with a hook as well as someone to catch dinner. I was beginning to wonder if I should start looking for nuggets in the stream myself, but I was preoccupied with the treasure that I could think about nothing else but finding it. I was going to change my strategy this time, though, and bring a metal detector. It had a setting on it for different metals, one of which was gold. While planning to go a few days before, I told Teddy, "We could have tested this metal detector in the backyard on your gold nugget if you hadn't of gone and sold it."

"Why don't you go and buy it back so I can find it again. Would that work okay for you?" he quipped.

I said with a chuckle, "No Ted, but it sounds like it would work well for you."

"Hell yah! Better yet, let's go up to that gulch and find a whole bunch more of those gold nuggets."

"You bet! We'll go and get them all. We'll show everyone how good we are at treasure hunting."

"Darn right." Teddy had that smug look on his face I'd seen many times through the years when he was darn sure that he was right about anything.

That same evening, Uncle Johnny called on the phone and said he'd like to come out and visit and asked me if I could take him back up to Flo's diner and Dead Man's Gulch. "Would you mind if I come back out for a visit? I want to see Flo and help you find that treasure that you've been looking so hard for."

I quickly said, "Hell no I wouldn't mind! It would be fun to have you come along again and I know I'd be safe from that darn old grizzly bear if you were there."

"Damn right you would be, Charlie." He couldn't stop laughing. "I can't get there until next Friday, though. Can you wait until then to go?"

"Sure Uncle Johnny. I'm sure Christiana's gold can wait one more week to be found after all these years."

After making arrangements to pick him up at the airport, I called Teddy to tell him the change in plans. He was elated to have Uncle Johnny come along with us. They were a pair of characters, alright.

Then I called Flo to let her know we would be coming by the following Saturday with Uncle Johnny. "All right. Good going, Charlie. I'll cook breakfast for you guys, okay?"

"Sounds great Flo, see you then." I acknowledged.

As the week went on, delaying the trip turned out to be a good thing. Sarah injured her foot chasing a raccoon out of the backyard. There was no way I was going into those mountains without Sarah. I had been nurturing a small fish pond in my backyard and for some reason that year the local population of raccoons had begun to think I was putting dinner out for them. In the first four years of having a pond full of fish, we had never had a problem with the raccoons. We raised goldfish to a good size. Meredith fed them by hand. We also had a catfish to keep it clean, a smallmouth bass, some baby trout, and Koi fish. After the first attack by the family of raccoons, I hired a company to catch and move them, but they couldn't catch the grandpa raccoon and he became troublesome.

I took the advice of one of Meredith's friends and went to the

Cheyenne Mountain Zoo to purchase what's called "Zoo Doo." It was actually tiger droppings and it costs twenty-five dollars a bucket. My in-laws still laugh about that. I went out and spread it in the backyard, feeling like a dummy. Then I waited on the back porch for mister raccoon. When he jumped over the fence, I was surprised to see him stand up on his hind feet and sniff the air, then turn and run like the wind the other way. I'll be damned—it worked! Until, that is, two months later when grandpa raccoon figured out there was no lion to go with the . . . you know what. That was the time Meredith let Sarah out for her morning yard prowl and mister raccoon found out there was something even bigger in our yard. Well, no worries. Her foot healed before the next Saturday when it was time to go. Since I had time off that particular Saturday, I decided to use it wisely and pick up where I left off on my research.

That morning during my visit to the Pioneers Museum, Leah and Kelly were helpful to me. I was able to find out that Fort Lewis had been ordered closed in 1891. It became an Indian school in 1892. The area where the fort was located is a place called La Plata. The school later became an agricultural school and moved to Durango to become a college. The area where it was located is now an experimental station. Okay, I thought, an Indian school. Mary was a translator. Her dad was a general at the fort before it closed. I wondered if she had gone back there after Maiku died. The time frame was just right. Now I was stopped dead in my tracks again until I could visit Durango and look for records of the Indian school. Research can be fun if it doesn't make you to dizzy. I wanted to go that very minute. The four-hour drive gave me second thoughts, but I wasn't going to let that stop me. I quickly went home to get Meredith's blessing to go, which she provided right away. Then I packed a change of clothes and started driving south to Canon City and then west to Montrose where I went south to Durango. I arrived just in time to spend an hour at the Durango Public Library. I went directly to the microfiche research area and began looking through Durango newspaper articles in the card catalog for the 1890s.

I had thought I was driving alone to Durango, but I now think I may have had Christiana along for the ride because I got lucky very quickly. Almost immediately, I found three newspaper articles concerning Mary Rivet. The first article read: *Major Rene Besaw to wed Mary Rivet at Fort Lewis School.* "A ceremony will take place Saturday night, November 17th, 1893 at the Ute school on Fort Lewis. Major Rene Besaw, Retired Army officer, will wed his lifelong friend Mary Besaw, a teacher at the school. Both were from Glens Falls, New York, where they met as children. The best man will be Major Besaw's son Raymond and the maid of honor will be Mary's daughter Philemon Louise." I was happy to have found them after all that effort. I was shocked and in disbelief, though. I had heard the name Besaw before. *It might be a coincidence*, I thought. No, it must be a coincidence that was my great grandmother's maiden name. I remembered Charlotte reciting the family history she had found in Glens Falls. Grandma always said she had Iroquois ancestors. I couldn't even imagine the slight possibility that I could be Christiana's great, great, great grandson. I tried to forget that and get on with my job before the library closed.

The second article announced several baptisms at the school. Included in the list of six children was that of Philemon Rivet, who received the baptized name of Louise. The date of the article' was September 2, 1892. Now everything made sense. I couldn't find anything about Mary and Philemon in Glens Falls because I was looking for the wrong names.

The third article finished my research at the library just in time for closing. It read: *Indian school announces retirement of teacher Mary Besaw. She will retire to her hometown of Glens Falls, New York with her husband, Retired Major Rene Besaw, son Raymond Besaw, and daughter Louise Besaw.* I drove back home that night. When I awoke the next morning, I showed the printed newspaper articles to Meredith and said, "I have to go back to Glens Falls."

"You sure do, Charlie."

"Do you think I could be Christiana's descendant?" I asked in disbelief.

"You could be, Charlie. Maybe your cousin Charlotte could help you with that. I do think you would want to find out why your grandma always talked about the Iroquois part of the family," she replied matter-of-factly.

"Okay, that's a good idea. I'll give Charlotte a call right now." My hands shook as I dialed the phone. When Charlotte answered, I said, "This is Charlie. You won't believe what I found out!"

"Well, what could that be, Charlie?" she wondered.

"There is a possibility that we are Christiana's descendants, she may be our great, great, great grandmother. First we have to find out a little more in Glens Falls to be sure," I said.

"You're kidding me, Charlie. Aren't you? What makes you think that?" she asked with a deep gasp of breath.

"I found some newspaper articles in the Durango Newspaper about the Fort Lewis Indian School. Christiana's son, Maiku, whose wife Mary Rivet went to the fort that her father had been assigned to. She became a teacher there when it became an Indian school and married Major Rene Besaw, whom she knew in childhood in Glens Falls. Her daughter Philemon became Louise when she was baptized and then became Louise Besaw when Mary married Rene. They then moved back to Glens Falls where grandma was from. Didn't you tell me from your research that grandma's mother's maiden name was Besaw? Was her first name Louise?" I asked

"Yes Charlie, that is right. I have also found a photograph of Grandma's mother, whom appears to look and dress like she was of Indian descent. What a great find Charlie." She was very happy.

"It could be Charlotte, but I'm puzzled about why grandma had always said that she was part Iroquois." I beckoned to her.

"I don't know about that Charlie. We will have to go back to Glens Falls and try to find out." She replied as if she was confident what the answer would be.

"I already have Meredith's permission to go, but Uncle Johnny is coming out here for next Saturday's trip to Dead Man's Gulch. It will have to be sometime after that." I hesitated.

"I can't wait that long Charlie. I will just go myself next Saturday and let you know what I find out." She insisted.

"Okay Charlotte, that sounds terrific. You're the best," I said with relief.

"Thanks, Charlie. I want to find this out as much as you do. I'll call you when I return from Glens Falls. Good luck on your treasure hunt and say hello to Uncle Johnny," she added.

"I will, and good luck to you. Talk to you then." I said goodbye.

CHAPTER NINETEEN

I was in an upbeat mood all of that next week. At night I
walked around the house talking out loud to Christiana.
"Am I really your great, great, great grandson, Christiana?"
I did not hear a reply, but somehow I knew she was listening
and smiling. On Friday night I went to the airport to pick up
Uncle Johnny. I wore a big smile. I'd been lucky and was think-
ing if my luck held up I might find the treasure of Dead Man's
Gulch.

"Hey Charlie, how are you?" Uncle Johnny asked cheerfully.

"I'm terrific, Uncle Johnny. I have some fun things to tell you
about." I smiled.

"Yah right, Charlie. You always have something fun to tell
about," he said, breaking into his familiar chuckle.

"I guess you're right about that, but this is really fun. I'll tell
you about it on the way back to the house," I assured him.

"Okay, but can we stop on the way for some cold ones?"

"Already have that taken care of, Uncle John. They're in the
fridge," I replied matter-of-factly.

"That's why I like to come to visit you, Charlie. You always
take care of the important things. I hope we have an easy trip to

the gulch this time. I don't want to hurt any grizzly bears," he said with a laugh.

"Me too, I wouldn't want any grizzly bear to hurt me," I sighed.

We both laughed. I told him about the research. That was the first time I had ever seen Uncle Johnny at a loss for words. It was only momentarily. He laughed and said, "Damn Charlie, you sure do live an interesting life. Hey, wait a minute! That would mean the treasure belongs to us, wouldn't it? Ha!"

"If we can find it, it sure does Uncle Johnny." I was happy, too.

"What are we waiting for? Let's go get it, Charlie." He replied with enthusiasm.

"Maybe we'll find it tomorrow, Uncle Johnny. Maybe tomorrow."

"Damn right we will, Charlie. Can we ask Flo to go with us?"

"Sure, maybe we'll ask Meredith to come too and take Mariah along. We can set up a picnic in the gulch." I said.

"Sounds good to me. I'll give Flo a call when we get to your house," Uncle Johnny said with a glow.

When we arrived home and asked Meredith to go, she thought it was a great idea. Uncle Johnny called Flo and she was very happy to go with us. She offered to provide the picnic lunch from the diner and we made our plans to pick Teddy up at 7:00 O'clock and then meet Flo about 9:30. We packed our gear that night and got breakfast early the next morning. The drive up Ute pass was beautiful. The temperature was just right and there was no more than a spot of a cloud hanging over Pikes Peak. Sarah had to sit in the far back of the Jeep and couldn't stick her head out of the window so we made an extra stop for her. That seemed to make her very content and she really loved having all of the people with us.

When we arrived at the Diner, Flo came out with a big smile and an extra big hug for Uncle Johnny. She gave a hug for Teddy too. "How is everyone doing?" She asked as she kept up that smile.

"Just great Flo, what did you pack for our picnic?" I asked hoping for some of her green chili.

"Roast beef sandwiches, homemade potato salad, chips, drinks and oh yah, Charlie, some green chili and tortillas for you. I also have some special apple sauce for the baby. Oh there she is, hello Mariah, you are so pretty. Hello Meredith, it is great to finally get to meet you." She said with a special genuine charisma that only she seemed to have.

"Hi Flo, I have wanted to meet the person who has always been one of Charlie's favorite people and has fed him so well," Meredith responded in kind.

"Looks like she's going to feed us all pretty good today," Teddy smiled big now too.

The six of us and Sarah packed tightly into the Jeep. Sarah begged Flo for what was in her lunch basket.

"Oh yes, and Sarah, I packed you some rib bones too." Everyone laughed. When we turned off the main road and entered the gulch, I stopped for a Sarah break and let everyone stretch. Meredith commented about how beautiful the scenery was. "This must be why the state is named Colorado; it really is colorful."

"Yes, that is the Spanish translation for the color red," I assured her. "Look at the Aspen trees turning green now."

"Yes, and they are so yellow in the fall," Meredith observed.

"This sure is a colorful place whenever Charlie comes here," Uncle Johnny added.

"I hope it's colorful with gold today." Teddy had to get a word in.

"Maybe we should all get going and find out." I was excited as I got back into the Jeep. All of the usual wildlife was out and about. There was also a big horn sheep I hadn't seen before standing on one of the rocky ridges.

As we parked and unloaded the Jeep, Teddy said, "I think I'll stop at my fishing spot and see if I can find another one of those gold nuggets."

"Good idea! I might just stop at my favorite spot for a couple more of those nuggets," Uncle Johnny added.

"Okay you guys, maybe Flo and I can take Mariah and the food to a good spot for our picnic. Does that sound good to you, Flo?" Meredith wondered.

"That sounds great, Meredith. What a beautiful day it is for a picnic."

I grabbed the metal detector out of the Jeep. "That sounds good to me, everyone. I'll just have another look around. Come with me, Sarah." I motioned to my companion and she happily came running.

I walked a short distance and looked for the circle Christiana spoke of in her diary. I heard Meredith yell out, "Charlie, we found a spot for the picnic! Come on over."

"I'll be right there," I said as I walked over to them.

"Look at the great spot we found for lunch. This rock is perfect for a table—and oh, look! It's in the shape of the moon!" Meredith said in delight.

"What did you say, Meredith?" I asked as my mind lit up with excitement.

"Charlie, look." She pulled back the tablecloth. "It's shaped perfectly—like the moon."

"That's it, Meredith. It must be."

"What, Charlie? It must be what?" Meredith asked.

"Christiana's moon, it is one of the clues. Look for a circle around here somewhere." I beckoned as I stepped back and away from the rock. I could see that the rock was on a slight slope which led up to the back of the waterfall. There seemed to be a small dry stream bed leading down from that hill and passed under the rock and down into the river. Walking further back I noticed some small piles of rock which did encircle the moon rock. That's when I knew.

"You found it, Meredith!" I yelled with delirious joy.

"I found what, Charlie?" Meredith asked, confused.

"The treasure! You found the treasure! It must be under that rock. Do you see the circle of piled-up rocks? Those must be the graves of the massacred men. Don't you get it? The circle of life and death!" I exclaimed.

"Holy cow, Charlie! It's so big . . . how can we possibly move it?" Flo asked.

"Uncle Johnny . . . Teddy! Come over here! I need your help." I couldn't believe they each came over with another gold nugget.

"What's so important, Charlie? I was getting rich over there," Uncle Johnny asked.

Teddy followed with "Yah Charlie, what's up?"

"Not much guys, just the treasure of Dead Man's Gulch. I think it is under that big rock." I assured them.

"If you say so Charlie, then let's get that thing moved." Uncle Johnny replied. We all got together and pushed that big old rock aside. Under it was a sunken hole where the water from the flash floods had passed through. I got down on my knees with my little camp shovel and began digging. I didn't have to dig very far when I discovered a hide of a deer or an elk. Everyone gasped.

"I'll help you pull that out of there Charlie." Uncle Johnny offered.

"I'll help too." Teddy offered as he stuck out his good arm.

We were all in total shock as we opened it. There was the gold. We found it. It had been wrapped in that hide for 120 years. There were gold nuggets galore. The water had worn a hole in the side of it though and some of the nuggets had washed out down into the stream. We didn't know how many, but we were sure that is where the nuggets that Uncle Johnny and Teddy had found came from. We were all jumping for joy. Mariah didn't understand at that early age what was so fun but she just laughed right along with everyone else. We counted 162 pieces of gold and admired them for a very long time. We all enjoyed our picnic immensely on that beautiful rock and just stared and admired all of that gold. "We better get going with the loot before we get company." I said with worry.

"Good idea." Uncle Johnny stuffed all of the gold into my backpack.

"Yah, we rich people had better get out of here," Teddy chuckled.

Awash in happiness, we packed up and drove out of the gulch. "I think it's time for a party." Uncle Johnny was certain. "Will you come with us to Charlie and Meredith's house, Flo?"

"You'd better believe it!" Flo was only too happy to comply. When we got back home, we stacked all the gold on the kitchen table and there was much joy and merriment. We didn't know how rich we all were, but I thought we might be very comfortable. My cousin Charlotte called at that time and had more good news. She'd found birth certificates and confirmed that Christiana was indeed our great, great, great grandmother. Louise Besaw married Robert "Moses" Rivers, whose mother was an Iroquois Indian. Just then, a light flickered on in the stairway. Christiana knew we'd found her descendants and I was one of them. Wow!

Uncle Johnny and Flo were married at the gulch in June and they live happily in Buena Vista. Sarah and I go on treasure hunts from time to time. Best of all, I get many visits, finally, from all of my relatives. They usually want to go to the river in the gulch where they too have found many gold nuggets.

Meredith keeps a dozen of fresh roses on the table in a bucket as a symbol of my good luck.

Coming Soon!

CHARLIE'S GHOST TOWN
By Ray Golden

CHAPTER ONE

Bullets flew through the air on Main Street in the Colorado town of Forest City. Men fell to the ground left and right. Troy Clark died in front of Mary O'Malley's Trading Post. Steve Kinney slid down from his saddle in front of Little Scott's livery stable. The front windows of Marilyn's General Store exploded as women and children took cover behind the counter. The saloon erupted into a brawl and Sam Starr's outlaw friends decided to join the fray. Hell had broken loose, and Sam was the culprit. Armed with a shotgun and a pistol, he was out to kill as many people as he could. Drunk again, he wanted revenge for being thrown out of town earlier that day. "I'll kill every one of you!" he yelled as he reloaded his guns. "Come on out here for your justice, cowards!"

"Drop those guns or I'll shoot you in the back, you miserable excuse for a husband!" Belle Starr demanded as she rushed out of Fanny Porter's boarding house. She and Sam had been hiding out there from Judge Parker in Fort Smith, Arkansas.

"Go ahead and shoot. I cannot die. I am a Cherokee. The spirit of the Great Bear will protect me from your bullets."

"I'm not fooling around, Sam. Drop those damn guns!" Belle again demanded.

Sam turned and fired. Belle ducked behind a porch beam. Just then, I felt pain in my left ankle. I went down, shot in the foot.

"What's the matter, Charlie? Wake up, wake up, you're dreaming!" My wife pleaded.

"I've been shot, Meredith," I gasped in pain.

"No, Charlie, you haven't been shot. You were dreaming," Meredith assured me.

"If I was dreaming, why does my ankle hurt so much?"

"Oh Charlie, have you been seeing ghosts again?" Meredith asked with deep concern. She was referring to my previous encounters with a ghost named Christiana, whom I'd learned was actually my great, great, great grandmother. I had discovered her past and my own destiny in my search for the lost treasure of Dead Man's Gulch.

"I guess so. I'm sure glad I was dreaming. It all seemed so real. I remember being a whiskey salesman back in the old west. I've always wanted to know what it would be like to actually be there." I replied.

"Yes, Charlie, but you'd better be careful where you go to

because you might not be able to get back." Meredith chuckled and rolled over. "Now please go back to sleep, Charlie. Tomorrow's a work day."

"Okay, but my ankle sure feels like that bullet was real," I moaned.

When I awoke the next morning, my ankle was still sore as if the dream was real. I wasn't dissuaded from still wanting to go back to the real old west, though. "Meredith, I want to take Sarah up to Forest City next weekend. I'd like to go into those old buildings to see what's there." Sarah was my Great Pyrenees dog who always accompanied me on mountain trips. She'd proven to be valuable on previous trips to Dead Man's Gulch.

"Charlie, haven't you already had enough excitement for one lifetime in all of those trips up to the gulch?" she asked with a smile.

"I guess so, honey, but I can't stop my curiosity." I replied with the boyish grin I wore when I laughed at myself.

"Okay Charlie, it's fine with me. I guess that's why I married you. Never a dull moment!"

The dream stayed in my memory for several days. Then I had another dream. I found myself strapped into a dental chair. A tall, thin man spoke to me. "You're damn lucky I was in town, stranger. I don't take kindly to strangers who interrupt my poker games. What's your name?" He had a stern edge to his voice.

"Ben. Benjamin Silver," I replied nervously.

"Well Ben, they tell me you're a liquor salesman. If that's true, this here operation is going to cost you one very good bottle of whiskey. Do you agree to my terms?" the man growled.

"But I only have one sample bottle left, sir."

"You only have one left leg too, Ben. Which would you like to keep, the leg or the bottle?" He stared at me with an *I got you* grin on his face.

"I'd like to keep the leg, doctor," I said with definite surety.

"You can call me Doc, Ben. I'm Doc Holliday." He broke into a great big grin.

"But I heard that you were a dentist," I wondered out loud.

"There isn't much difference between pulling teeth or bullets, Ben. Now hold tight," he sneered.

When the bullet had been removed, Doc put it in a jar and looked over at me. He knew I was relieved. "You might want to keep this for a souvenir, Ben. You're a brave man. Now where exactly is that bottle of whiskey?" Doc asked without breaking a single bead of sweat.

"It's over there in my coat pocket, Doc," I replied with relief.

"It was nice doing business with you, Ben. If I find the son of a bitch that shot you, I'll get even for you." His voice had an edge of sincerity.

Suddenly, Meredith woke me with a stir. "Where were you this time, Charlie?"

"Forest City again, I think. I was in a dentist chair and Doc Holliday took a bullet out of my ankle. The year was 1886 on the calendar I stared at on the wall," I explained.

"Well, I'll say one thing for you Charlie, when you dream, you sure do dream big," she said in amazement.

"But that's the strange thing, Meredith. I don't think I was dreaming. I think I was remembering a past life."

"Now Charlie, you know I've got an open mind, but that's a little hard to believe." She shook her head.

"I'm sure it is hard to believe, but what I'm telling you is true. I think my encounters with Christiana have opened some kind of psychic door to my thoughts and I'm having flashbacks of a previous life."

"Okay Charlie, when you put it that way, it makes perfect sense. It's been thundering and lightning tonight. I think we were having a storm the other night when you were dreaming. I wonder if the electricity in the air had anything to do with your dreams," she wondered.

"It could be, Meredith. It feels like a door opens and suddenly I'm there," I described.

"I guess that could be right, Charlie, but please don't get shot again." She wasn't joking.

"Okay, but I don't think I can change what's already happened," I said.

"Go back to sleep now, Charlie. You have one more work day and then you can take your trip to Forest City on Saturday with Sarah," Meredith reassured me.

"That sounds great. I can't wait to go." I released a sigh. The next few days I day dreamed about my upcoming journey. I had one more dream, though I didn't mention to Meredith. It left me with a dark and scary feeling in my guts. I remembered two brothers who were a part of a large family from old Virginia. I thought that they were my brothers. The oldest was Davy. He was a strong-willed and physical presence of a man in the 1800s. He led many wagon trains on their way out west. The second brother was Daniel. He was a clever and crafty survivor who had worked as a detective for the Pinkerton agency. I could not remember any more specifics than those. At the end of my dream, one of the brothers was missing. He was there one moment and gone in the next. That feeling of insecurity stayed with me until my thoughts became so crowded that this particular thought took a back seat to all of the others.

Early Saturday morning, I packed my Jeep with all of the supplies and gear that experience always told me I might need. Sarah sat patiently at the front door. She always knew when she was going for a ride. I never knew a dog more intelligent than her. Meredith waited in the hallway and watched to be sure that I had all of the needed supplies. Our three cats, Milkbox, Bobo, and Annabelle, wondered what the commotion was all about. They sat in a row like a king flanked by two princesses. Our one-year-old baby girl, Mariah, sat up on her blanket on the living room floor and smiled at her little kitties. Meredith expressed concern about the weather forecast calling for storms. "There might be thunderstorms up there today. Please be careful and don't take a nap. I don't want you to have any of those dreams up there in the wilderness."

I laughed. "Don't worry about that, I don't think there's any shooting in a ghost town, honey."

"You never know about those things when you're around,

Charlie," Meredith said with the wily smile she wore on special occasions.

I drove up Ute pass along with Sarah, her huge, happy head hanging out the rear window. I noticed Aspen trees beginning to turn the beautiful gold color they are famous for. A slight fall breeze was in the Colorado air and few clouds hovered over the crest of Pikes Peak. Tourists on the highway waved and laughed at Sarah as they turned off in the direction of Old Colorado City and Garden of the Gods. As was often the case, the temperature cooled by the time we reached Green Mountain Falls. The smell of wood burning in a nearby fireplace permeated the mountain air. I passed several mountain bike riders from the nearby Olympic training center. They struggled mightily to negotiate the steep and curvy road. It would take nearly three hours to arrive at our destination. Yet it didn't seem so long with the awesome view afforded to us by the view of the Colorado Rocky Mountains. Over the back of Pikes Peak and past Florissant is a mountain prairie with a view forty miles ahead to the great mountain range of the Continental divide. Florissant is a mountain town known for its dinosaur fossil beds. Sarah barked as we both gazed at a herd of buffalo which were now being bred and raised on a private ranch to the west of Lake George. Elk mingled among the buffalo. I spotted an eagle flying above a rocky knoll with the ease provided by a slight breeze. A short time after, we saw two bighorn sheep enjoying the sun at the top of a nearby rocky hilltop.

When we closed in on Buena Vista, I stopped and gave Sarah

a rest break. As I let her out of the back of the Jeep, I noticed the remains of a rock slide strewn across the dirt road which was adjacent to the scenic rest area. "I'm sure glad that we weren't here for that, Sarah," I said to her. It was my habit to talk with her just like she was another person. She thought that she was a real person, too. She acknowledged me by lifting her foot, as if to shake hands. Once she was back in the Jeep we continued the final leg of our journey to Forest City.

Arriving at the base of the Mosquito Mountains, I noticed a dirt road with an old wooden sign which read *Forest City: Last stop before heaven.* As I turned off and drove through the thick Aspen trees, I felt as if I was traveling back in time. Little did I know then that was exactly what was happening. The dirt road was washed out in many places and I was pleased to have a vehicle that could negotiate the ups, downs, and holes in the road. The remains of long-ago-abandoned railroad tracks tilted on the slope of the adjacent hillside. Now I could see the buildings. Wow, there were fourteen in all!

The first building on the right was a little school building. It had a small porch out front with a bell still hanging from its center post. I stopped there first to look around. I found an old wooden sign on the ground. It read *Shelley Dumas School.* I wondered what she was like. I was able to open the front door and go in. I could almost hear the kids laughing. Little furniture was left though, except for a table and two broken chairs. Sarah came in behind me and barked. I followed her out just in time to see a female mule deer and her two button fawns scamper away.

I decided to leave the Jeep and walk through town. There wasn't a person anywhere. Sarah and I were alone, but yet, not lonely. I felt comfort as if I were at home. We stopped to sit and enjoy the roast beef sandwiches Meredith had packed for us. Yes, Sarah got a sandwich too. I dozed off for a minute, and then awoke in a startle from Sarah's loud bark. I saw and heard nothing, but knew something was amiss. Sarah must've sensed or heard something. After a few moments of silence, I asked Sarah to come along as we went exploring again.

The next building we came to was the tallest in town. It had three stories and porches on the front of each. The paint had long worn off and an old kerosene lamp lay broken on the front porch next to the remains of a bench. Above the door was a faded carving which read *Kathleen Melanson Boarding House: No snoring.* Somehow I knew she meant it. Going inside, the front desk blocked my entry like a security guard. Dust caked the whole of the place. An old register was left on a shelf under the top counter. Faded names and dates with room numbers crowded the pages. I thought that it might be okay to give this abandoned remnant a home and tucked it inside my backpack. Just then I changed my mind. I sat in the corner and took the book out of the backpack.

My curiosity got the best of me. I wanted to know who had stayed there. I couldn't read many of the names, but among those I could read on the first page were Buck Saybrook, Harvey Clinton, Lisa Putnam, Darlene Danielson, May Summers, Geraldine Ashford, and Dusty Pomfret. The date on the top of the page was May 5, 1886. That was the day Kathleen had opened for business. An inscription at the top read, *First Day: Heaven help me.* As I skimmed through the pages, I recognized names, both famous and infamous: Sam and Belle Starr, Doc Holiday, Leroy Parker, and Wyatt Earp. Two more familiar names were recorded: Daniel and Davy Silver. An eerie feeling overcame me as I noticed writing that looked just like my own. I didn't think anyone could ever write as badly and unique as I did, but there it was. The name was Ben Silver. That was the name I'd had in my dreams. How could this be? Was I dreaming again?

At that moment, flashes of lightning sliced through the darkened sky outside. *Crack! Boom!* The deafening sound of thunder followed the fierce lightning. Hail and rain came down hard on the building. Sarah hugged me closer as I shielded her from the onslaught. The hair on my arms and Sarah's brow stood on end from the electricity in the air. I was surprised at the quickness of the incoming storm. That is the moment that my dreams turned into reality and my reality turned back into the dream.

I felt lonely, but not alone now. Someone else was with me. I was sure of it. As I looked upward toward the staircase, a vision became all too real. A woman was coming down the stairs humming a song. I was astonished. She was dressed in a long, woolen dress edged with lace. An apron hung from her waist. Just then, she looked directly at me. I knew she could see me. "Why are you sitting on the floor, Ben? Your ankle must be hurting. Do you want some help back up to your room?" I got up off of the floor to answer. As a second thought, I turned to be sure I was still there—or the person I thought was me was still sitting there on the floor. Then, in an instant, I became Ben Silver again with the full knowledge of who that person frozen in time was and his dog, too. Sarah was still with me and yet with him too. "Hi White Bear, how are you today?" She asked my large, shaggy white dog as she patted Sarah on the head.

"Good morning, Kathleen. You're your usual cheery self this morning. Yes, my ankle's very sore. I was just letting White Bear out for her morning break. I can make it back up to my room, but first I want to go over to Debra Montana's saloon and thank Doc Holiday for taking that bullet out of me," I told her.

"Okay Ben, but I'd wait a while if I were you. Doc's in a foul mood this morning. Gizzy Howard tried to cheat him at poker last night and Doc had to shoot him in a fair gun fight. Gizzy drew his gun first and Doc shot him while steely-eyed. Sheriff Dawson was sitting nearby and attested to the fairness of the fight. They hauled Gizzy out to Sherman's cemetery this morning and buried his cheating body along with the crooked deck of cards he used. It's a good thing for you that Doc decided to stop at Forest City on his way from Pueblo to Leadville. Doc told me yesterday his good friend Wyatt Earp was going to stop here and see him on his way to Denver." Kathleen hummed again and walked back into the kitchen.